MOSAIC
OF FAITH

PIECING TOGETHER OUR CHRISTIAN STORY

EVERETT LEADINGHAM, editor

Though this book is designed for group study, it is also intended for personal enjoyment and spiritual growth. A leader's guide is available from your local bookstore or your publisher.

BEACON HILL PRESS
OF KANSAS CITY

Editor
Everett Leadingham
Assistant Editor
Jeremy Coleson
Senior Executive Editor
Merritt J. Nielson

Copyright 2007
Beacon Hill Press of Kansas City
Kansas City, Missouri

ISBN: 978-0-8341-2286-4
Printed in the United States of America

Cover Design
Chad A Cherry
Interior Design
Sharon Page

10 9 8 7 6 5 4 3 2 1

CONTENTS

1 **The New Testament Church**
(1st Century) by Stan Ingersol 5

2 **Justin: Martyr and Apologist**
(1st-3rd Centuries) by Diane Leclerc 15

3 **Augustine: Amazingly Graced**
(4th-5th Centuries) by C. S. Cowles 23

4 **Monasticism: A Rule of Life**
(6th-11th Centuries) by Stan Ingersol 33

5 **St. Francis: Of Beggars and Cathedrals**
(12th-14th Centuries) by C. S. Cowles 43

6 **Martin Luther: Gripped by Grace**
(15th-16th Centuries) by Carl Leth 53

7 **Jacobus Arminius: A Question of Character**
(17th Century) by Carl Leth 61

8 **John and Charles Wesley: Love Aflame**
(18th Century) by C. S. Cowles 71

9 **Francis Asbury: An Offer of Myself**
(18th-19th Centuries) by Floyd Cunningham 81

10 **Phoebe Palmer: Holiness Matriarch**
(19th Century) by Diane Leclerc 91

11 **Phineas Bresee: In All Things Charity**
(Early 20th Century) by Floyd Cunningham 101

12 **The Emergence of Evangelicals**
(Mid-20th Century) by C. S. Cowles 109

13 **The Present Religious Landscape**
(Late 20th Century) by Stan Ingersol 119

THE NEW TESTAMENT CHURCH

(1ST CENTURY)
BY STAN INGERSOL

C. H. Dodd, a New Testament scholar, believed that the crucifixion and resurrection of Jesus at the heart of Christian preaching makes Christianity a deeply historical religion. If Christians are going to claim that God was revealed in history, then history must be taken with utter seriousness.

We might even say that history is indispensable to Christian faith. Indeed, we might say that the Christian faith is historical or it is no true religion at all.

Christian roots lie deep in the hopes and aspirations of ancient Israel, but the Christian story finds its focus in the history of one particular man—Jesus of Nazareth—a Galilean born during the reign of Augustus, the first Roman emperor, and executed by imperial soldiers in the reign of the second emperor, Tiberius.

The life and teachings of Jesus are at the core of Christian belief and practice. That Jesus was raised from the dead by God's power was evidence for the disciples of a divine seal upon His teachings that give them authority. Furthermore, His resurrection is a pattern for the resurrection of His disciples.

Thus, Christian belief and practice arise out of the *very stuff* of history.

AN IMPORTANT WRITER

A single writer known as Luke wrote one-fourth of the New Testament.

Bible scholars refer to Luke's original work as "Luke-Acts." They do so because his composition is widely believed to have originated as a single piece of literature that combined a Gospel (a work about Jesus' life, teachings, death, and resurrection) with an account of the apostolic era.

Luke's intention was to give a written witness to the rise of the Jesus movement of the first century. His account begins with Jesus of Nazareth, continues with the formation of the Christian *ecclesia* (church) in Jerusalem, and recounts the spread of the faith into the nations known today as Syria, Turkey, and Greece. Luke-Acts is a long work richly populated with many characters, but its towering figures are Jesus, Peter, and Paul.

After Luke-Acts circulated, the Christian church later divided Luke's work into two separate "books" so that the Gospel portion could take its place in the canon (or the authorized list of Scriptures) alongside the other Synoptic Gospels (Mark and Matthew), with which it shared striking similarities. The other portion—Acts—was then placed after the Gospel of John to form a bridge within the canon between the four Gospels and the Epistles of Paul that followed.

Throughout this chapter, we will refer to Luke's original composition as "Luke-Acts." We will do so in order that Luke's original intention and the full scope of his work is always in our minds.

WHO WAS LUKE?

As a rule, we know very little about the various New Testament writers, except for Paul, whose letters disclose many key facts about him, as does Luke-Acts. In most cases, we're not certain of the writers' actual names. Luke's writings never divulge his name either. But early Christian tradition attached Luke's name to the composition, and there is no reason to doubt it. Across the centuries, Bible commentators have generally assumed that some references in the Pauline letters and the "we" passages in later chapters of Luke-Acts refer to Luke the writer. If these assumptions are correct, then several details about Luke emerge.

First, at the end of his letter to Philemon, Paul conveys greetings from a circle of his close friends: Epaphras, Aristarchus, Mark, Demas, and Luke (Philemon 24). At the close of his letter to the Colossians, Paul adds greetings from the exact same circle. Colossians provides an additional detail: Paul refers to "our dear friend Luke, the doctor" (Colossians 4:14). These references identify Luke and the others as Paul's associates at these points in Paul's ministry.

Luke-Acts fills out more of the picture. In three distinct passages, Luke-Acts shifts from "they" language to "we" language—apparent references to the writer's own participation in the events he describes (cf. Acts 16:10-17; 20:5—21:18; 27:1—28:16). These passages indicate that Luke joined Paul's band at Troas (on the west coast of modern Turkey) and traveled with them to Philippi in Greece, where Luke then remained. When Paul returned to Philippi several years later, Luke rejoined the company of travelers for Paul's journey east to Jerusalem. After Paul's imprisonment in Caesarea, Luke accompanied him on the journey to Rome. Thus, Luke is associated broadly with Paul's mission to the Gentiles, with the church at Philippi, and with Paul's imprisonment.

The identification of Luke as a physician has captured the imagination of novelists and has been reflected across the centuries in Christian art. When Eastern Orthodox and Western art depict the Four Evangelists (Gospel writers), Luke is often shown holding a symbol of the healing arts.

To learn more about Luke, we turn to his writing. His literature bears the stamp of its author's mind and thought.

LUKE SETS TO WORK

Luke addresses his work to Theophilus. The name means "Lover of God." Theophilus may have been the name of an influential member of the Christian community, perhaps even Luke's patron. Or "Theophilus" may be a literary way of commending the work to anyone who loves God and searches honestly for truth. If the latter is the case, then it is addressed not only to Christian seekers of the late first century, but also to us today.

It is important to pay attention to Luke's methods, for they shed light on the formation of the New Testament.

Luke is clear about his approach to writing: his work is one of systematic research. He has consulted written and oral sources, and drawn on his own experiences as an associate of Paul. He reveals these methods at the beginning of Luke-Acts. He notes how "many have undertaken to draw up an account of the things that have been fulfilled among us, just as they were handed down to us by those who from the first were eyewitnesses" (1:1-2). Luke is stating clearly that the first sources of information used by early writers about Jesus and the Early Church were the oral traditions "handed down to us."

Further, these oral traditions were set down into an orderly account by "many." Then he adds: "I too decided, after investigating everything carefully . . . to write an orderly account" (v. 3, NRSV).

The passage bristles with implications. Who were "the many" who wrote these "orderly accounts"? The Gospel writer Mark was surely one of these whom Luke had in mind, but we do not know the names of the others. By the time Luke wrote, probably around the year 80, some of these accounts may have already been consolidated. Luke's choice of words suggests his personal knowledge of some of them.

New Testament scholars have identified two of the written sources that Luke knew and relied upon for writing

Luke-Acts. Mark's Gospel is one of these. Luke and Matthew both incorporate Mark's short Gospel into the outlines of their own longer Gospels. Mark, used as it is by Luke and Matthew, is widely regarded by biblical scholars as the first of the four Gospels to be written. The material that Luke (like Matthew) draws from Mark's Gospel includes narrative sections, parables of Jesus, and aspects of the Passion story.

Another document used by Luke and Matthew in their Gospels has no name attached to it, so Bible scholars simply call it "Q"—the first letter of the German word for "Source" *(Quelle)*. This common source used by Luke and Matthew is a collection of Jesus' teachings. Luke and Matthew arrange the sayings in somewhat different ways in their respective Gospels. The Sermon on the Mount in Matthew and the Sermon on the Plain in Luke are a clear example of this. Both writers clearly draw on this source to convey to readers and hearers the content and moral strength of Jesus' teachings.

Finally, there are verses in Luke that appear only in this Gospel and no other. These passages may include material from some of "the many" accounts that Luke acknowledges preceded and stimulated his own careful investigation.

Did Luke also have written sources for the Acts portion of Luke-Acts? We do not know. There are no other early histories of the apostles to compare his account with, but nonliterary sources are evident. First, the "we" passages allow us to conclude that some details in Acts were drawn from Luke's personal experience, while others were drawn from his conversations with Paul and others whom he encountered as he traveled in Christian circles. His knowledge about the Jerusalem Council (Acts 15), for instance, may be shaped by conversations with participants in that event.

To summarize, Luke utilized a variety of sources to write Luke-Acts: oral traditions, "orderly accounts" written by earlier authors, conversations with participants in key events of New Testament history, and his own experiences.

LUKE'S DISTINCTIVE UNDERSTANDING OF CHRISTIANITY'S RISE

Luke-Acts is unified by a number of distinctive themes. We can only discuss a few of them.

Two themes are closely related: Luke's emphasis on the universality of the gospel, and his emphasis on the Holy Spirit's active role in the life of Jesus of Nazareth and in the emergence and spread of the apostolic church.

As Luke tells the story, the Holy Spirit is manifested in the lives of John the Baptist and his family (1:15, 67), in the conception of Jesus (1:35), and in the old man Simeon's prophecy that the infant Jesus carries the "salvation, which you [God] have prepared" (2:30-31). The Spirit descends upon Jesus at His baptism (3:21), leads Him into the wilderness (4:1), and later to Galilee (4:14) to begin His public ministry. In Nazareth, Jesus reads from the Isaiah scroll, then proclaims: "The Spirit of the Lord is upon me, because he has anointed me to bring good news to the poor" (4:18, NRSV).

The same Holy Spirit who propelled Jesus' ministry likewise drives the ministry of the Early Church. Jesus promises that the disciples "will receive power when the Holy Spirit comes on you" (Acts 1:8). This promise is fulfilled on Pentecost, when the disciples are "filled with the Holy Spirit" (2:4) and witness boldly to Christ's resurrection (2:14ff). In his Pentecost sermon, Peter declares that the prophet Joel's prophecy has been fulfilled: "In the last days, God says, I will pour out my Spirit on all people" (2:17).

Luke takes particular care to underscore the Holy Spirit's role in the spread of Christian faith to new groups. The Holy Spirit calls Philip to explain Scripture to the Ethiopian eunuch (8:29), and is manifested when Peter preaches and baptizes in the household of the Roman centurion Cornelius (10:44-47) in Caesarea. Luke emphasizes the Holy Spirit's work in crossing one social barrier after another and reaching new groups of people. Likewise, the Spirit works through the missionary efforts of Paul, opening some doors to his ministry and closing others (16:6-7). For Luke, the same Holy Spirit that propelled Jesus' mission also propels the spread of the gospel, including (and especially) the mission to the Gentiles.

Luke's writing also calls special attention to God's particular love toward the poor and others who are socially marginalized. The theme is pronounced in The Magnificat, Mary's song, where the mother of Jesus praises the child growing in her womb and proclaims: "[God] has brought down rulers from their thrones but has lifted up the humble. He has filled the hungry with good things but has sent the rich away empty" (Luke 1:52-53).

In Nazareth, Jesus identifies the beginning of His mission with a passage from Isaiah that says the Spirit of the Lord had sent Him "to preach good news to the poor . . . to proclaim freedom for the prisoners . . . to proclaim the year of the Lord's favor" (4:18-19). The "year of the Lord's favor" was "jubilee," a year in which all financial debts were canceled.

Throughout the centuries, this "mission statement" of the Lord has been appropriated by those of His disciples who have especially ministered to the poor. John Wesley closely identified the mission of early Methodism with this statement. Many others have identified with it, including William and Catherine Booth, The Salvation Army founders; Orange Scott, the Wesleyan Methodist founder; B. T. Roberts, the Free Methodist founder; and Phineas Bresee, the primary Nazarene founder.

The theme continues throughout Luke's work. In Acts, the members of "First Church" Jerusalem—the church founded at Pentecost—held "everything in common" (Acts 2:44), and the order of deacons was established so that no one would be left out of the distribution of food (6:1-5). Luke's writing consistently emphasizes God's love toward those who are pushed aside by the rich and powerful.

AN ENDURING INFLUENCE

Luke-Acts does not tell the whole story of early Christians. Luke writes nothing about the Jesus movement's spread into Egypt, where a strong and influential church developed in Alexandria, a regional capital of the Roman Empire. Nor does Luke write about the spread of the faith into the East, where it likewise took root. His focus is on Galilee, Judea, Samaria, Syria, Asia Minor (Turkey), and Greece—the parts of the story that he knew.

Luke's role in Christian history has been critically important. Imagine how impoverished the New Testament would be without his contribution to it. Imagine only three Gospels and no account of the early spread of Christianity except for the details gleaned from Paul's letters. Without Luke's work, the New Testament would be very different indeed.

We often think of historians as simply chroniclers of events, but Luke assumes a larger role than that. History is memory. And memory is a matter of absolute importance in the construction of identity. A person with no memory has no identity. Memory is what ties a person's past and present together, and it shapes a person's future.

Yet, memory not only shapes persons; it shapes groups and communities. Without a shared memory, there is no communal identity either.

Doug Newton, Free Methodist writer and editor, states that people will invent a history when they do not know their own, for they must have a past, even a fictional one if necessary. In his perceptive address, "The Importance of Recital," Newton calls attention to Psalm 78:2-4. Reciting "things from of old—what we have heard and known, what our fathers have told us"—the very things that in turn "we will tell the next generation" —was significant in shaping the Israelites into a faithful community that stood in continuity with its past.

Luke's significance to the Christian story is very similar.

Luke was a catcher of memories, of stories of God's actions in human history.

His friend Paul was a great missionary to the Gentiles and the Early Church's first great theologian and ethicist. And Luke had a portion in that mission.

Still, his towering contribution was Luke-Acts. As copies of Luke-Acts began circulating in the late first century among the Christian groups, it began shaping their communal identity. And it has shaped every generation of Christians that has come since then.

Scripture Cited: Psalm 78:2-4; Luke 1:1-3, 52-53; 2:30-31; 4:18-19; Acts 1:8; 2:4, 17, 44; Colossians 4:14; Philemon 24

JUSTIN: MARTYR AND APOLOGIST

(1ST-3RD CENTURIES)
BY DIANE LECLERC

In the first three centuries of Christianity, the Church developed its identity in important ways. These include (1) its identity in relation to the Roman Empire and (2) its self-identity in working out its essential beliefs. In other words, these centuries are marked by the persecution of Christians by the Roman government, and by the fine-tuning of the Church's theology as it began to recognize persons and ideas in their midst that misrepresented the gospel.

MARTYRDOM

Early on, Christianity was perceived by the Romans as a Jewish sect. This gave it a type of toleration from the Roman Empire, for it was granted the same liberties as "Israel." But as Christianity slowly began to be seen as a "new religion," the Empire took notice—it was only as Christianity began to be perceived as a separate sect that the persecutions began to mount. As early as A.D. 64, representatives of the Roman government (in this case, Nero) saw the new religion as dangerous to Roman peace.

In the second century, the persecution of Christians was often sporadic and regional. Local governments would persecute for specific reasons. Some of the most famous of these were the persecutions and martyrdoms in Lyons and Vienna in 177, and in North Africa in 202 and after. These persecutions are recorded for us as savage and horrific. Christians were killed by wild animals and by gladiators; they were beheaded, sliced to pieces, or burned. When Decius became Emperor in 249, the local persecutions became empire-wide. He required that all Christians sacrifice to the Roman gods. If they did, they received a certificate of obedience. If they refused, they would face punishment, even death. Later, Emperor Valerian forbade Christian meetings, ordered the clergy to sacrifice, and put to death any that declined. However, the worst persecution was still to come.

In 284, Diocletian came to power. His rage against the Christians was even more aggressive. He ordered that all churches be demolished and that any Scriptures be confiscated and burned. Christians were forbidden to assemble; clergy were imprisoned. Any Christians found in the higher ranks of society lost their social and legal status—if not their lives. Any Christians who refused to deny Christ and sacrifice to the gods were executed. Many persons were tortured and martyred during Diocletian's reign.

Throughout Christian persecution, those who did not give in, but chose to die for their faith, became the heroes of Christianity. Their deaths (called their "birthday") were celebrated liturgically as feast days very early on. "Martyr" literally means "witness;" and as one Early Church father stated, "The blood of the martyrs [was] the seed of the Church." It was true that many persons watched the Christians under the conditions of impending torture and martyrdom and were converted by the courage and faith they saw. The martyrs were the truly holy ones, according to the Church. They were seen as the persons who rightly shared in the "sufferings of Christ" (1 Peter 1:11).

One of the early martyrs was a man named Justin. His attempt to argue against persecutions by writing directly to the emperor makes him an important Early Church figure. Also very important is the strategy he used when writing, called "apologetics." Only when a later emperor acknowledged Christ (Constantine in 312) did the persecution of Christians stop.

JUSTIN THE MARTYR

Justin was born at the turn of the first century, near the year 100. All that we know about him comes from his own writings. He was born in Flavia Neapolis, which was formerly called Sichem in Palestine. His parents were most likely pagans. He received a good education, which meant that he studied philosophy extensively. He began as a Stoic—a type of philosophy that emphasized the goal of being in control of all of one's passions or emotions. Later on, he was strongly influenced by the philosophy of Plato, which dominated the thoughts and culture of that day. This Platonism would become a key to his understanding of Christianity.

Justin was dramatically converted around the year 130. The story says that as he walked along the seashore (perhaps in Ephesus), Justin met a man who convinced him that he could not think or reason himself to God. This man told him about the Old Testament and how it prophesied about Jesus Christ. Justin later remarked that all he had been searching for in philosophy he found in Christ. His lifelong quest for truth led him to Christianity. We know that he was a teacher for the rest of his life, in Ephesus and in Rome, where he led his own Christian school. He was finally condemned to death in the year 165. We are told that he, along with six of his friends, were scourged and beheaded for refusing to sacrifice to Roman idols, thus the name Justin *Martyr*.

Between 150 and 160, Justin Martyr wrote several important works. In his first *Apology*, he outlined a reasoned resistance against the charges that were being brought against Christians. There was no basis for the government's condemnation, he said. After that, he wrote a second *Apology*, as well as other papers that show his theology in more depth.

There were three main issues that Justin tackled in this first letter: (1) Christians were being accused of atheism because they would not recognize the gods of Rome. Justin, of course, defends the God of Christianity as the only true God worthy of worship. Christians were not atheists at all! (2) Christians were suspected of cannibalism! This is an obvious misunderstanding of the nature of the Lord's Supper. Non-Christians had heard the language of eating the flesh of Christ and drinking His blood, and interpreted it quite literally. Justin explains Communion as a symbolic celebration in order to refute such charges. And (3) Christians were condemned for child prostitution.

This last accusation is not as obvious as the first two charges and takes a bit of explanation. It was common for some of the mystery religions of the day to raise children from an early age with the designation of becoming temple "virgin" prostitutes, believing that relations with these children was an act of worship. This is obviously hugely immoral—so much so that even the Roman government condemned the practice. Coincidently, it was also a common practice by this time in the Christian community for some young adults to remain celibate, or "virgins," in service of the Church. These are the earliest roots of a longstanding Christian tradition of monasteries and convents. Justin had to address how different Christianity's purpose for these young people was from the evil intention of the mystery religions.

Justin's ultimate defense of Christians was an appeal to truly investigate their *character*. If they were unethical, then punish them accordingly; but do not, Justin argued, punish them only for wearing the name "Christian." Unfortunately, there is no evidence that Justin's appeal to the emperor had any effect on the persecutions. Christians continued to be persecuted for the next 150 years simply because they claimed Christ as Lord, as the Holy One to be worshiped.

DOCTRINAL ESSENTIALS AND CHRISTIAN APOLOGETICS

The second important aspect of self-identity developed as disagreement grew about what "true" Christians believed. Whose teaching should be followed? What criteria should be used in order to weed out false beliefs? Numerous interpretations of Hebrew scripture were arising; what was the correct interpretation? Who was Jesus Christ? Who was the Holy Spirit? What was their relationship to God? What new writings should be considered as part of a "new testament"? The Church's theology had been passed down from the apostles to teachers who taught the next generation, and so on. But what if false teachers also claimed to be part of the apostolic theological lineage? The need to clearly state and write down Church "doctrine" became extremely important.

Irenaeus of Lyons was the first to use the word "heresy" (around the year 175). He was opposed to the teaching of Valentinus, a Gnostic who was leading Christians astray. Gnostics believed, among other things, that the earth and creation are evil; that Jesus did not have a real human body; and that the "special knowledge" of salvation was given only to a few. Nevertheless, Gnostics considered themselves to be the true Christians! How were others to combat them? Irenaeus was really the first who drew a line in the sand and declared that Gnostics stood outside the Christian circle.

This led to the obvious—but up until that point little-acknowledged—need to articulate accurately and thoroughly Christian beliefs. Why were Gnostics "heretics"? What constituted true Christian faith? The Gnostics were also using parts of what was yet to be called canonized Scripture (the canon was not established until late in the fourth century). On what basis can Christians claim to know the truth? Irenaeus's work can be seen as an early attempt to answer these important questions, and to more clearly state them to a non-Christian audience. His method is known as "apologetics."

JUSTIN THE APOLOGIST

If we hear the word "apologetics" today, we will most likely define something like "a reasoned defense of Christian truth." Yet, this is only a partial definition of what apologetics meant in the Early Church. It is true that Justin defended the Christians, arguing that they did not deserve the harsh and often deadly treatment they received at the hands of the Romans. However, Justin did more. He also attempted to "witness" to Emperor Antoninus Pius and his sons by making connections between their world of ideas and his beliefs. He tried to create a bridge so that they could understand each other more easily. Unfortunately, we often neglect this openness to dialogue when we do apologetics today; too often we just build our forts to defend and protect ourselves. Justin was trying to find common ground for the purpose of affecting the emperor's soul, even though he was in danger for his own life. In essence, apologetics in the Early Church was not a defensive stand, but a form of loving evangelism.

Justin Martyr respected the emperor's, and especially his son Marcus Aurelius's, comprehension of philosophy. Marcus has been considered a philosopher himself. The mutual language that they understood was Platonism. Justin used this language in order to communicate effectively. Who is Jesus Christ? Justin knew full well, but how could he explain clearly to those who had no knowledge whatsoever of what Christians believed? Justin moved into their world in order to convey the gospel in ways that were accessible to them.

The famous philosopher Plato had, hundreds of years earlier, talked about a grand Communicator that represented the Divine Being to humanity. He called this ambassador figure the "Logos." In fact, when John's Gospel begins with the words, "In the beginning was the Word, and the Word was with God, and the Word was God" (1:1), he is using the Greek word "Logos." "In the beginning was the *Logos* . . ." Thus, John was speaking to an audience that understood the philosophical tradition of Plato. What John did that is so radical and stunning was to identify the *Logos* as Jesus, and to tell us that He became "flesh" and "made his dwelling among us" (v. 14). In a very similar way, Justin used the philosophy that the emperor would have understood, and also named the *Logos* as Jesus Christ.

Justin, still trying to work it all out logically, offered reasons why Plato could have been so prophetic, in a way, by conceiving of this divine ambassador. One of the theories Justin offered is that Plato had read the Old Testament! We have no evidence at all that this is true, but it is an interesting way of explaining the similarities between Platonism and Judeo-Christianity.

A second theory is much more compelling, particularly to Wesleyans. Using Plato's philosophy, Justin talked about a "divine spark" that is in every person. This divine spark allows each person to glimpse truth, even crave for truth. According to Justin, it is really the true *Logos*, Christ, that spreads out through all humanity and gives us an internal desire to seek after God, and the ability to see (if only unclearly) real truth. God has given all persons the ability to perceive what is true in the world. Put simply, we do not need to be Christian in order to understand that 1 + 1 = 2. Or, to express it another way, all truth is God's truth. God is the author of all that is true. He gives all humans access to certain degrees of reality.

What Justin was conveying is a very early expression of the doctrine John Wesley called "prevenient grace." Besides what is explained in the above paragraph, this doctrine also primarily gives us an explanation of the fact that even before we seek God, God is calling or "wooing" us. God is seeking to communicate with us, and so the first thing He does is give us an internal ability to hear Him! We could not sense this without God working in us. Wesley and Wesleyan theologians identify this grace as the work of the Holy Spirit.

Justin actually lived before the doctrine of the Holy

Spirit was fully worked out. (This happened gradually, but the First Council of Constantinople in 381 was the event that confirmed and affirmed that the Holy Spirit is an active part of the godhead.) Justin was attempting to explain why Plato, who pre-dated Christ, perceived and expressed ideas similar to Christianity. Justin attributed this to the "spark" of Christ that spreads out through all humanity in all times and places—what we would call prevenient grace and the work of the Spirit. Justin found the Platonic idea of the *Logos* helpful in his explanation. So then, Justin used a Platonic idea to communicate a Christian belief. Again, his purpose was to convince the emperor, just as Justin himself had been convinced, that Christianity is the "highest philosophy" and that it provides the answers to all of our questions.

It is perhaps important to say in conclusion that while apologetics can be an effective witnessing tool in its attempt to give evidence and logical argument as to why one should believe in God and Christ—using reason as its primary tool—becoming Christian still requires a leap of faith. As the man who witnessed to Justin said so well, we cannot think ourselves to God. Not that Christianity isn't based on facts, but ultimately, it is the Holy Spirit that works in our hearts with these facts to bring us to real trust in Christ for our salvation. In the end, Justin was much, much more than a Christian philosopher. He was faithful to the point of being willing to die as a testimony to his love and loyalty to Jesus. Justin, philosopher and apologist, died as Justin Martyr. Through the blood of such persons, the Church has expanded throughout the centuries and throughout the world.

Scripture Cited: John 1:1, 14; 1 Peter 1:11

AUGUSTINE: AMAZINGLY GRACED

(4TH-5TH CENTURIES)
BY C. S. COWLES

Tortured in mind and heart, Aurelius Augustinus sat weeping in the garden of his friend Alypius. Like a tender sapling straining to lift its head toward the light of the sun, he found his heart yearning for the peace and assurance of his godly Christian mother, Monica. On the other hand, he was bent low under the weight of guilt over having taken a mistress with whom he had a son out of wedlock. He had often prayed, "Grant me chastity and continence—but not yet."

On this summer afternoon in A.D. 386, he heard children singing, "Take up and read." Seeing a scroll of Paul's Epistle to the Romans lying on the bench beside his friend, he opened it and read, "Let us behave decently, as in the daytime, not in orgies and drunkenness, *not in sexual immorality* and debauchery, not in dissension and jealousy. Rather, *clothe yourselves with the Lord Jesus Christ,* and do not think about how to gratify the desires of the sinful nature" (13:13-14, emphasis added).

He did not need to read any further, because a clear light flooded his heart and all his doubt vanished. In that transformative moment, a sensitive soul and towering intellect was born into the Kingdom and would have a monumental impact upon subsequent Church history.

A HISTORIC TURNING POINT

On October 28, A.D. 312, a half-century before Augustine's birth, a most important battle was fought. Face-to-face with his strongest rival, Constantine, whose father Constantinius had refused to carry out Emperor Diocletian's orders to kill Christians, had a dream. In it, he saw a cross in the heavens that shone brighter than the sun. Above it was the inscription, BY THIS SIGN, YOU WILL CONQUER.[1] Hastily, he had crosses painted on his helmet and the shields of his soldiers.

Shortly after his victory over Maximus, the newly crowned emperor of Rome issued the "Edict of Milan" legalizing the Christian faith. Thus, three centuries of sporadic, but often severe, Roman persecution of the Church came to an end. With Constantine's conversion to Christianity, the Church suddenly found itself transformed from a harassed minority to the status of Rome's most favored religion. That was the good news.

The bad news was that the Church was drawn into a fateful partnership with imperial Rome that would have dire consequences down to our own day. The simplicity that characterized the Early Church's worship morphed into the pomp and ceremony of the imperial court. As the religion favored by the emperor, the Church grew at an astonishing rate. Many of the new members, however, had experienced no real transformation of life and moral character. It was not long before the Church lost its sharp edge, and began to mirror the pagan culture of its day, especially its lust for wealth and power. The world desperately needed a spark that would once again light the flame of vital New Testament Christianity, so God raised up Augustine.

FORMATIVE YEARS

Aurelius Augustinus was born on November 13, 354, in what is now Algeria. By his own admission, he was even in childhood a liar and a thief. He tells how he and some other boys stole some pears from a neighbor's tree even though they didn't like pears. He later confessed that he took joy in the theft and in the sin. He saw this as evidence of the intractable depravity of unredeemed human nature.

His mother sent him to school as a young boy. He fell in love with learning, and read the Greek poets and philosophers with relish. Even as the passions of the flesh burned in his youthful body, so did the fevers of the mind. He threw himself into the study of Latin, rhetoric, mathematics, music, and philosophy. After a short stay in Rome, he moved to Milan to prepare for a career in law. It was there that he fell under the spell of Bishop Ambrose, a powerful preacher who became to him the father he felt he never had.

Augustine and his friend Alypius were baptized by Ambrose on Easter Sunday, A.D. 387. He broke off his relationship with his mistress, and moved to North Africa. He planned to establish a monastery where he could pursue a quiet life of holiness. A small, Catholic congregation in neighboring Hippo, however, needed an assistant for their aging Bishop Valerius. One day when he went to the church to pray, worshipers seized him, drug him to the altar, and forcibly ordained him as their priest. When Valerius died, he was appointed bishop of Hippo, and remained there until his death in A.D. 430.

He who had sought a life of unobstructed contemplation now found himself in a whirlwind of ceaseless preaching, pastoral duties, and writing. His literary output was phenomenal. Four hundred sermons and 200 letters—some very lengthy—have survived, as well as numerous books, two of which have exerted enormous influence down to our day.

His most popular work, *Confessions,* pioneered a new form of spiritual autobiography, much imitated by Christian and secular writers ever since. He was a profound analyst of the human spirit, particularly looking at one's self. He felt far from God, as if his life were a waste. Deeper still, however, was his "hunger and thirst for righteousness" (Matthew 5:6), and his determination to center his life in God. He weaves his confession of sins, struggles with intellectual problems and theological heresies, and spiritual breakthroughs into a beautiful tapestry. His passionate longing for God is given succinct but profound expression in his most often cited prayer, "Thou hast made us for thyself, and our hearts are restless until they rest in thee."[2]

At the very time when the Goths and Vandals were marching through the gates of Rome in A.D. 410, bringing down the curtain upon the "eternal" Roman Empire that had endured for nearly a thousand years, Augustine was putting the finishing touches on one of the classical masterpieces of Western literature, *The City of God*. In it, he contrasts the earthly city—the state—with the city of God—the Church. While the former is built upon a love of self, the latter is founded upon love for God. Though believers live out their lives in the earthly city, yet they are called to place their faith in the kingdom of God, which unlike Rome and all earthly empires, will never pass away (see Hebrews 11:10).

THEOLOGICAL CONTRIBUTIONS

From the time of his baptism, Augustine was drawn into the fiery furnace of theological disputes. The controversies that consumed so much of his time and energy proved to be the anvil upon which four major theological insights were hammered out, three of which became cornerstone doctrines of Christian orthodoxy. The first was *the nature and source of evil*. The major question of his time had to do with theodicy: that is, how can a God who is at once all-powerful and all-loving permit evil? The Manicheans' response was that two eternal beings control the universe, one good and the other evil. Though the all-good deity is superior, he cannot at present overcome the evil one. They believed, as the Gnostics before them, that all that is visible, physical, and temporal is evil, and that which is invisible, spiritual, and eternal is good.

Against this "cosmic dualism," Augustine developed an idea he believed to be consistent with biblical revelation: namely, evil is not a "thing" or "substance" intrinsic to matter, but rather is the loss of good. Evil is to goodness what darkness is to light. The source of evil is not to be found in anything material, but in the misuse of human freedom, an evil will. John Wesley captured the essence of Augustine's insight when he defined sin as a *willful* transgression of a *known* law of God.[3]

Second, it was Augustine's confrontation with the schismatic Donatists that drove him to spell out a *clear doctrine of the Church*. Bishop Donatus, alarmed over the increasing worldliness of the Church and the corruption of its popes, withdrew from the Church, taking many with him. Believing that the sacraments could be administered and the grace of God found only in an undefiled church, they organized their own.

Augustine agreed that the Church exists as a mixed institution. It includes not only those who are worthy, but renegades. The sacraments, however, are ordained by God, and their efficacy is not dependent upon the character of those who administer them, but upon the Christ honored in the consecrated bread and wine. More serious than moral vileness, he believed, was the lack of love shown by people like the Donatists, whose judgmental spirit sowed seeds of contention and schism.

Third, out of Augustine's ongoing debate with Pelagius came his *doctrine of original sin*. Pelagius, a devout British monk, believed fervently in the freedom of the will. There was something more "original" than original sin, according to Pelagius, and that was original righteousness. While Adam's fall set a bad example—and, admittedly, almost everyone had followed him into sin—it did not destroy the innate capacity of human beings to freely respond to God's gracious call and to keep His commandments. After all, Pelagius reasoned, why would God issue commandments impossible for people to obey? Humans are born not only with freedom to sin, but freedom to *not* sin.

Not so, said Augustine. Drawing largely on his own failed attempts to live a chaste and holy life, he argued that the corruption of human nature due to Adam's sin renders humans incapable of doing anything but sin. Only the supernatural power of God's grace—imparted through baptism, according to Augustine—can break the stranglehold of sin and restore genuine human freedom. Grace and holiness cannot be achieved by an act of the will, but only received as gracious gifts of God in the obedience of faith. Only then do believers have both the will and the power *not* to sin.

Finally, toward the end of his life Augustine wrote *On the Predestination of the Saints*. In it, he brought predestination into the center of theological discourse. One of the burning questions of his day was why so few who hear the gospel respond in believing faith. Augustine believed that God "elected" those few to be saved, while the rest were left to their deserved condemnation. Why some are chosen and others are not lies in the hidden determinations of God. This was one of his doctrinal contributions that the Church did not embrace and largely ignored for a thousand years, until John Calvin resurrected it and made it the cornerstone of the enormously influential *Institutes of the Christian Religion*. The oft-repeated evangelical mantra, "God is in *total* control," is a succinct statement of Calvin's doctrine of divine determinism. It is a position that not only attributes everything to God, be it good or evil, but makes no room for the freedom of the will.

A FATEFUL COMPROMISE

For more than three centuries, Christians believed that the call to follow Christ was a commitment to nonviolence.

They were so sure of this that they would rather die than fight, and did so by the tens of thousands in wave after wave of Roman persecution. They abhorred bloodshed and refused to serve in the military. They believed that Christ had called them, not to conquer but convert, not to fight but forgive, not to destroy but heal. Armed with no rhetoric other than the gospel of peace and no weapons but love, these followers of the Prince of Peace survived in Rome without drawing a sword.

That changed, however, with Constantine's conversion. His edict of A.D. 381, making Christianity the official religion of the Roman Empire, meant that the well-being of the Church merged with that of the Empire. Consequently, Christians felt compelled to fight in its defense. Augustine went further. He conscripted Roman soldiers to force schismatic Donatists to return to the Catholic church or die. To justify reversing three centuries of nonviolent teaching and practice, he formulated the Church's first *doctrine of a just war.*

Tragically, once unleashed, swords wielded by Christians began to cut a wide and bloody swath across subsequent world history right down to our own day. As recently as 1994, Rwanda, the most heavily evangelized country in Africa with over 85 percent of its adult population baptized Christians, descended into an orgy of self-destruction. During 100 days of terror, over 800,000 Tutsi and Tutsi sympathizers were cut to pieces by the dominant Hutus. Jesus warned, "All who draw the sword will die by the sword" (Matthew 26:52).

LASTING LEGACY

Naturally, we desire to attribute infallibility to towering intellectual and spiritual giants of the past to whom we continue to look for guidance and inspiration. If ever one deserved the Catholic appellation of "saint," Augustine certainly qualifies. All are agreed that he was the most influential personality in the history of the Church, after the apostle

Paul. Yet, infallible he was not. Even as we could wish that Paul had been more forceful in his condemnation of slavery and less ambiguous about the role of women in home and church, so we could wish that Augustine would have made a larger place for free will in his doctrine of salvation, and would not have compromised Jesus' gospel of peace. If the law of unintended consequences has ever proven true, it is in the divisive and destructive effect that Augustine's stance on these two issues has had across the centuries.

That, however, does not diminish the inestimably positive influence Augustine has had upon subsequent Church history and theology. *First,* thanks to the candor and transparency of his *Confessions,* we can drink deeply from the well of a truly great soul. For 1,500 years, believers have found their minds enlightened and spirits nourished.

Second, we cannot grapple with any significant theological issue without asking, "What did Augustine have to say?" A quick check of the index of any major theological work shows how indebted we are to his rigorous thinking. We may not always agree with him, but we cannot ignore him.

Third, he was uncompromising in his fidelity to the truth revealed in Christ, embodied in the historic creeds of the Church, and affirmed through the rigorous application of critical thinking. He would have none of the "sloppy agape" that marks so much of today's warm-fuzzy, seeker-friendly, "let's affirm everybody" climate of unconditional acceptance. Religious pluralists are fond of saying, "There are many paths up the mountain." Augustine understood, however, that some doctrinal paths lead us off the edge of a cliff. All we have to do is recall the mass suicides of nearly a thousand of Jim Jones's followers in 1978, and the deaths of the Branch Davidians in the Waco fire of 1993. Augustine reminds us that sound doctrine matters.

Fourth, Augustine's fateful use of the military serves as a cautionary tale of the folly of trying to bring in the "kingdom and his righteousness" (Matthew 6:33) by coercive means. While we are called, in both testaments, to be responsible citizens and to "seek the peace and prosperity" of whatever "city" we find ourselves (Jeremiah 29:7), we should not forget that we are, first and foremost, "a chosen people, a royal priesthood, a holy nation, a people belonging to God," and consequently are "aliens and strangers in the world" (1 Peter 2:9, 11). Our salvation is to be found not in any political ideology, but in God.

Finally, over against the inevitable drift of earnest believers across the centuries toward legalism, Augustine pleasantly reminds us that our salvation is not an achievement resulting from our rigorous efforts, but "is the [gracious and unmerited] gift of God" (Ephesians 2:8). Great joy and freedom comes with discovering that *there is nothing we can do that will make God love us more;* and *there is nothing we can do that will make God love us less.* Augustine is a worthy model of what it means to be "amazingly graced."

Notes:

1. The Latin for this phrase is, "In hoc signum, vinces." Today, we often see the letters "IHS" on crosses, standing for "in hoc signum."

2. Maria Boulding, *The Confessions* (St. Louis: Faithworks, 2002), 4.

3. *Letters, The Complete Works of John Wesley,* vol. 12 (Albany, Oreg.: AGES Software, 1996, 1997), 452.

Scripture Cited: Jeremiah 29:7; Matthew 5:6; 6:33; 26:52; Romans 13:13-14; Ephesians 2:8; 1 Peter 2:9, 11

MONASTICISM: A RULE OF LIFE

(6TH-11TH CENTURY)
BY STAN INGERSOL

The call to holiness is embedded deep in the Scriptures. "Come out from them and be separate, says the Lord" (2 Corinthians 6:17). In the Old Testament, this call was intended to give Israel a distinct identity rooted in Torah obedience to the one God.

Jeremiah introduced the idea of a "higher righteousness," of a day when God's law is written on peoples' hearts. Jesus and Paul developed this theme further in the course of their ministries.

From the earliest days of the Church, Christians have answered this biblical call to holiness in many different ways. They have also had different understandings of what separateness from the world entails.

Monasticism is one way that people have answered the call to holy living. But even within the ranks of the monks, there have been different ways in which "separation from the world" has been conceived and lived.

VISION OF THE DESERT FATHERS

The roots of Christian monasticism lie in Egypt and Syria, where "the desert fathers" of the second and third centuries sought refuge from worldliness by cutting themselves off from ordinary society.

For the most part, these first monks were solitaries, living in individual isolation. They renounced life in the world and practiced a strict asceticism. They fasted and prayed. In early Christian allegory, the desert was regarded as the abode of demons. So, the monks who went into the desert regarded themselves as soldiers who were invading the demonic habitations and engaging in spiritual warfare against the tempter and his legions. They were determined, by God's grace, to achieve spiritual victory by overcoming the world, the flesh, and the devil.

Anthony (251-356) was the best known of these. Born in Egypt, he sold his inheritance at age 20 and became a hermit. An older man tutored him initially; but in time, Anthony moved deeper into the desert. For two decades, he lived in isolation near the Red Sea. Then in about 300, he reappeared as a spiritual teacher. He attracted disciples who lived near him and accepted him as their spiritual director for longer or shorter periods of time. Some of these disciples, in turn, moved elsewhere and became teachers of monastic discipline. It is estimated that thousands of monks lived in Egypt at Anthony's death, many of them inspired by his example and teaching. Athanasius of Alexandria, one of the great bishops of the Early Church, wrote and published *The Life of Anthony,* an influential writing that attracted followers in both the Greek-speaking East and the Latin-speaking West to monastic living.

The whole notion of living in total solitude, though, was severe. It overlooked a primary human need: connection with others. Pachomius, too, lived originally as a hermit, but he concluded that a new form of monasticism was needed. It should be social in nature. He believed that monks needed community and accountability in order to best live lives separated to God. He gathered monks into a community in southern Egypt. This new form of social monasticism began to flourish, and monastic communities developed for women as well as men. The communities supported themselves through their own labor. Life as a community had to have organization, and Pachomius is credited with developing the first monastic "rule." His rule outlined the monastic community's daily schedule, including common meals and common prayer. These new type of monks were known as cenobites (KEN-o-bites).

Egyptian monasticism had a profound influence beyond that nation's borders. The monastic movement, in both its hermetical and cenobite forms, spread throughout the Mediterranean world—to Palestine, Syria, Anatolia (modern-day Turkey), and beyond Asia Minor into Greece, Italy, and the western reaches of Europe.

JEROME AND THE CALL OF SCHOLARSHIP

The life of Jerome exemplifies the interaction of eastern monasticism and western culture. Born in Dalmatia (in eastern Europe) in 341, Jerome exhibited a scholarly bent early in life. He was sent to Rome to study. There, he mastered the subjects of classical education: grammar, rhetoric, and literature. He lived for a while in Trier, Germany, where he developed an interest in Christian literature. There, he also developed an interest in the virtues of the self-disciplined life and in contemplation.

Later, he moved to Antioch in Syria, where the mission to the Gentiles had been launched three-and-a-half centuries earlier. There, Jerome began a systematic study of the Greek language. In the late 370s, he lived in Constantinople, studied with other scholars, then returned to Rome to serve as an assistant to Bishop Damasus. In Rome, he produced a Latin translation of the New Testament.

After Damasus's death, Jerome returned to the Middle East, settling in Bethlehem. Two monasteries were founded there—one for men and another for women. Jerome headed the first; his friend, Paula, headed the second.

From his monastery in Palestine, Jerome produced a

Latin translation of the Old Testament and a series of commentaries on various books of the Bible. His Latin translations of the Old and New Testaments are known as the Vulgate Bible; and in the Latin-speaking West, this was used as the authoritative version of the Bible throughout the Middle Ages. After the Protestant Reformation, it remained the authoritative text in the Roman Catholic Church for several more centuries; the Reformers beginning with Luther, however, began fresh translation projects that replaced Jerome's work in the new Protestant communions. Jerome's insights into the biblical text were also influential, and his commentaries were consulted throughout the medieval period and, later, by the Protestant Reformers.

Jerome was not flawless. He was opinionated and temperamental. He was not the first scholar-monk either, but he *was* the most famous one. To later monks, Jerome epitomized the idea that Christian scholarship was a compatible facet of monastic life. His blend of piety and self-denial, coupled with his scholarly achievements, inspired the idea that monasteries and convents should be places of intellectual achievement as part of devotion to holy living. And while not every monk could be a scholar, a monastery could be a place of learning.

BENEDICT'S ACHIEVEMENT

Benedict never commanded an army or exercised secular power, yet he had a profound effect on both Church and culture. Sometimes hailed as the father of Western monasticism, the very culture of Europe's Middle Ages felt his influence. Even centuries later, when Europeans settled the Americas and Roman Catholic missionaries planted their churches in Asia and Africa, Benedict's influence spread through the proliferation of Benedictine monasteries throughout the world.

Benedict's name means "blessing." It is from the same

source as our word "benediction"—the word of blessing with which we close our worship. His life spanned roughly the years 480 to 550. He was born into a well-known family in Nursia, about 70 miles northeast of Rome. He was sent to Rome to be educated, but he was appalled by the loose morals there. Eventually, he withdrew to Subiaco, a region about 40 miles away, where he took up residence in a cave and lived as a hermit. In time, he attracted disciples who sought him as their spiritual director. He began organizing them into monasteries around Subiaco. Eventually, there were 12 monasteries, each with a dozen monks and a local leader—an abbot. All were under Benedict's general authority.

According to an ancient source, a priest in the area tried to discredit Benedict. This in itself was sad, but indicative of a tension that occasionally existed between local pastors and the abbots of local monasteries. Pastors have sometimes resented the influence and respect accorded to abbots, who exerted influence on an area's wider religious life, but were completely independent of the pastor's influence or control.

Benedict left Subiaco and headed south, where in 529 he founded a new monastery at Monte Cassino, between Naples and Rome. He lived there until his death. Sister monasteries were planted, including one for women headed by Scholastica, Benedict's sister.

Like Pachomius and others before him, Benedict developed a rule to guide his monasteries. *The Rule of Benedict* became the most widely used one in Western monasticism. While he never set out to establish a monastic order, the wide adoption of his rule by other monasteries eventually led to just that. The Order of St. Benedict would eventually be joined by other monastic orders—the Dominicans, the Franciscans, the Augustinians, the Jesuits, among others—but throughout the Middle Ages, *The Rule of Benedict* would be more widely followed than any of those developed by the founders of other religious orders. And Benedictine monasticism would come to play an important role in the social fabric of Western Europe.

Two things need to be said about Benedict's rule.

First, it was not entirely original to him. Benedict was a student of the monastic literature that preceded him. While there are original elements in his rule, he drew upon earlier monastic rules and synthesized the elements that appealed to his philosophy of the holy life. He drew particularly upon the *Regula Magister,* or *Rule of the Master,* which was not much older than Benedict, and whose author is completely unknown to us.

Second, our interest is not so much in the details of Benedict's rule, but in its basic philosophy and in Benedict's concept of holy living which undergirds the rule.

Benedict not only believed that monasteries should be self-supporting; he also believed that daily work is an important part of the life of holy living. Through daily labors, the Christian interacts with others, is productive, and carries out the commandments of God.

Still, labor is only part of the bargain. The Christian should also worship God daily. *The Rule of Benedict* really made physical labor subordinate to worship. The worship schedule was primary, and the physical labor of the monastery was fitted around the schedule of worship, which Benedict considered the truest, highest, and most vital form of doing the *opus Dei,* or "work of God."

The monk's daily schedule, then, was rhythmic, see-sawing back and forth between periods of worship and work. The monks gathered together several times a day for joint worship. Other times in the day were devoted to solitude, where monks prayed or meditated alone. Between these times of worship, they performed their assigned tasks— working in the garden, cooking, or in the scriptorium where manuscripts were copied. Perhaps each day's alternating rhythm between work and worship can be understood as the Christian's coordinated use of both the right and left hands.

RULE AND DISCIPLINE

In 1991, the Order of St. Benedict and the World Methodist Council sponsored a joint conference on Benedictine and Wesleyan spirituality. The papers presented there delved into the spiritual practices of each tradition.

While the notion of "a rule" is basic to monastic life, Methodism also began with a notion of daily discipline. John Wesley's rules for the Holy Club at Oxford University, the first Methodist society, included daily devotions and prayers, fasting until 3 P.M. on Wednesdays and Fridays, visiting the sick and imprisoned, and taking Holy Communion once a week. Later, when the Methodist revival was under full headway, Wesley created rules for the burgeoning Methodist societies. Those rules gave structure and cohesion to the societies and moral direction to individual Methodists. For individual Methodists, Wesley enunciated the General Rules, which every Methodist was to follow. The General Rules were: (1) do no harm by avoiding evil in every form; (2) do good to the bodies and souls of others; and (3) attend all the ordinances of God, including public worship, the Lord's Supper, preaching services, and fasting. Wesley elaborated on each of the three General Rules.

A clear survival of the notion of disciplined life is found in the very name that the book of order carries in most Wesley-related denominations. While a few denominations refer to their book of order as a *Manual,* most refer to theirs as *The Discipline.* And while *The Discipline* today primarily sets out denominational structures, the name reflects the origins of Methodism in the methodical and disciplined Christian life.

BENEDICT IN THE 21ST CENTURY

A renewed interest in Benedict developed in the 20th century, and the term "Benedictine spirituality" was increasingly in vogue in some quarters as the century wore on. And this interest has appeared among laypeople as well as clergy, among Protestants and Catholics alike.

In the United States, for instance, there are today several thousand laypeople, representing many denominations, who are Benedictine oblates. A page on the Order of St. Benedict web site defines an oblate as "a lay or clerical, single or married, person formally associated to a particular monastery. The Oblate seeks to live a life in harmony with the spirit of Saint Benedict as revealed in the *Rule of Saint Benedict* and its contemporary expression."[1]

Why this broadened interest?

It has appeared mainly in industrial societies. It is partly in reaction to the modern workplace's mechanization, routinization of labor, and mass-production mentality. It is also a reaction to some of the dominant messages of our age. Modern advertising, for instance, seems to emphasize two basic messages: that we are primarily consumers who need material goods for fulfillment, or that we are primarily sexual beings who need to wear designer clothes (or do something else) to be more hip and more sexually desirable.

For the modern Christian, our social context provokes a compelling question: Who am I, really? And who is actually writing my life story? Is the script of my life story being written largely by economic forces and pop culture over which I have no control, or do I have a say in writing it as well?

The revival of interest in Benedict is tied directly to this concern. His emphasis on life's rhythm and the importance of worship in the ordinariness of daily living strikes a chord in the hearts of people who want to be more than what the economic system or contemporary pop culture tells them they should be. Benedictine spirituality is about priorities, especially the priority of putting God first. It is about re-ordering our lives. Those who learn from the way of Benedict blend prayer with their work. They strive for balance in their everyday life.

In *Soul Feast,* writer Marjorie Thompson emphasizes the importance of "a rule of life" for modern people: "A rule of life is a pattern of spiritual disciplines that provides structure and direction for growth in holiness. When we speak of *patterns* in our life, we mean attitudes, behaviors, or elements that are routine, repeated, regular. . . . It is meant to help us establish a rhythm of daily living, a basic order within which new freedoms can grow."[2]

We are not all called to be monks, but all of us are called to be thoroughly Christian. Indeed, we are called to be Christians all day long, every day of the week. Weekly church attendance is not enough. How can we learn from Benedict's emphasis on the daily pattern of spirituality?

Even in the modern workforce, most Christians can take a few minutes a day to pray the Lord's Prayer, and do so with a contemplative mind-set, not just as rote recitation. We can also take a minute and recite the Apostles' Creed in our minds, contemplating it as we do so—reminding ourselves, as we go through each sentence of it—*who* we are and *whose* we are.

There are other prayers and recitations that each of us can find that are short, meaningful, and easy to memorize. Saying and praying these throughout the day can help us stay focused on the things of God, remind us of how our public words and attitudes reflect upon our witness to Christ, and keep us in the rhythm of God's work through us in the world.

Notes:

1. <http://www.osb.org/obl/index.html>, accessed July 8, 2006.
2. Marjorie Thompson, *Soul Feast: An Invitation to the Christian Spiritual Life* (Louisville, Ky.: Westminster John Knox, 1995), 138.

Scripture Cited: 2 Corinthians 6:17

ST. FRANCIS: OF BEGGARS AND CATHEDRALS

(12TH-14TH CENTURIES)
BY C. S. COWLES

Tormented by tension between the self-indulgent life he was living as the privileged son of a wealthy Assisi merchant and the call of Christ to a life of self-giving service, Francis Bernardone came upon a repulsive leper on the road. Normally, he gave them a wide berth. On this day, however, impelled by a surprising surge of compassion, he sprang from his horse, embraced the filthy beggar, and emptied his purse into the man's disfigured hands.

As he mounted his horse and began to ride on, the heavens opened. Such joy flooded his soul that he could scarcely contain it. The die was cast. He would follow Jesus. He turned back to thank that leper for being the occasion for such spiritual rapture, but could find him nowhere. Down to his dying day, St. Francis of Assisi believed that it was none other than the risen Christ clothed in the diseased flesh of a leper that he encountered on that deserted road.

St. Francis, in his life before and after his conversion, personified the tensions that characterized the church of the High Middle Ages. On the one hand, it was a time when it enjoyed unprecedented influence, wealth, and power represented in magnificent cathedrals being built all over Europe. On the other hand, one of the most remarkable features of this era was Mendicant (beggars) orders of monks who not only took vows of chastity, poverty, and obedience, but lived by begging. It is between these extremes of ecclesial power and apostolic poverty that the story of the Church during these three centuries is framed.

PAPAL EXCESSES

Rarely has the proverb, "He who has the gold makes the rule," been more evident than in the Catholic Church of the High Middle Ages. Through all of the social, cultural, and political upheavals in which Europe had been embroiled since the fall of the Roman Empire, the church had filled the vacuum to become the most stable and dominant institution. It reached its pinnacle of influence with Innocent III (c. 1160-1216), who reigned as the most powerful pope in history. He deftly controlled kings and princes through the threat of excommunication. He made the papacy a strategic economic and trading force, and greatly increased the wealth of the church by collecting taxes from both clergy and laity.

Innocent III exercised virtually dictatorial control over every aspect of the church's life through its clergy, who alone could absolve sins and administer the sacraments. The doctrine of transubstantiation, actively spread by Innocent III, claimed that the consecrated bread and wine became the actual body and blood of Christ. Thus, to withhold the sacrament from communicants would be to deny them their only means of spiritual sustenance and grace. This became known as "the power of the keys," that is, the church hierarchy exclusively held the keys of the Kingdom in their hands.

To solidify his grip on power, Innocent III instituted the Pastoral Office of Inquisition. Its mission was to expose and destroy any who might represent a threat to the church's doctrinal purity and ecclesial power. It quickly became one of the most cruel and heinous institutions of coercion that the world has ever seen. Across the next six centuries, the inquisitors' rack, sword, and flame would consume hundreds of thousands of supposed heretics, infidels, dissenters, social misfits, and malcontents.

Spurred by the Mosaic Law "Thou shalt not suffer a witch to live" (Exodus 22:18, KJV), a witch-craze swept 16th- and 17th-century Europe. During that dark time, nearly 100,000 women—most of whom were single, poor, and social misfits—were put to death. They could be arrested and indicted on the uncorroborated testimony of one person, even a child. They were then "examined" by inquisitors who extracted farfetched confessions through the use of intimidation and torture. They would then be tried and convicted in a court of law, without the benefit of defense counsel or priestly ministration, paraded through the streets to be spat upon by a bloodthirsty populace, and finally subjected to the cruelest sorts of public execution.

The inquisitors' net also swept up those deemed to be a threat to the church's authority and teaching, such as John Hus (c. 1369-1415). Taking advantage of his platform as a university president, he provoked the ire of powerful prelates by preaching against immorality among the clergy, corrupt popes, and a church hierarchy consumed with lust for wealth and power. More than a century before Martin Luther, Hus declared that the Bible, rather than popes and church councils, should be the final authority in all things related to the faith. Hus not only believed that the laity should have access to the Scriptures, long forbidden by the church, but that they should be able to read the Bible in their own languages. For these "heretical" teachings, Hus was burned at the stake.

Boniface VIII (c. 1234-1303), the last of the 13th-century popes, tried to enforce Innocent III's principle of "one flock under one shepherd" by excommunicating Philip, the French king, for not abiding by his dictates. Philip retaliated by having the Vatican attacked and Boniface imprisoned. Although the pope's allies freed him, Boniface died within a month thereafter, partly because of the rough treatment he had received while in captivity. Never again would popes wield Innocent III's level of political power.

THE CRUSADES

The crusading spirit fired the imaginations and dominated the lives of Europe's Christians throughout the 12th and 13th centuries. Pilgrims had long journeyed to the Holy Land as a means of doing penance for their sins. They resented the fact that their holy shrines were in the hands of Muslims. Consequently, when Pope Urban II preached a fiery sermon in 1095 calling the faithful to free the Holy Land, they responded enthusiastically. To all who would fight, he promised indulgences to lessen their time in purgatory; and for all who died in battle, instant glorification as Christian martyrs.

Thus, the first of eight Crusades was launched. It cut a bloody swath of pillage, destruction, and land-grabbing across southern Europe, Asia Minor, and the Holy Land. The First Crusade, begun in 1096, was the most "successful." The slaughter, however, was horrendous. Justifying their brutality by citing the text, "Cursed be he that keepeth back his sword from blood" (Jeremiah 48:10, KJV), women were raped, cities were destroyed, and whole populations were exterminated—including defenseless women and children.

While Muslim and Jews were their primary targets, the crusaders were ordered, as they marched through southern France, to convert or destroy the Cathari, the "pure ones" (also called Albigenses), who rejected the authority of the corrupt church hierarchy. In their passion for holiness, they adopted strict ascetic practices, refused to bear arms, and would not kill either humans or animals. Refusing to defend themselves, they were mercilessly cut down by the crusaders' swords. After one of their cities had been captured, the conquering general inquired of the papal representative how they were to distinguish between the Cathari and good

Catholics. "Kill them all," he responded, "God will know which are His."[1]

The crusaders captured Jerusalem in 1099. Raymond of Agiles reveled in what he witnessed after Christian soldiers overwhelmed the defenders and swarmed into Jerusalem:

> Some of our men (and this was more merciful) cut off the heads of their enemies; others shot them with arrows, so that they fell from the towers; others tortured them longer by casting them into the flames. Piles of heads, hands, and feet were to be seen in the streets of the city. . . . So let it suffice to say this much at least, that in the temple and portico of Solomon, men rode in blood up to their knees and the bridle reins. Indeed, it was a just and splendid judgment of God, that this place should be filled with the blood of the unbelievers, when it had suffered so long from their blasphemies.[2]

The crusaders' victories, however, proved to be short-lived. The Muslims recaptured Edessa in A.D. 1144, inciting a Second Crusade, and drove out Jerusalem's Christian defenders in A.D. 1187, which precipitated a Third. Neither these nor any that followed succeeded in recovering Jerusalem or regaining the territory won during the First Crusade. The only enduring "success" they had was in driving Muslims out of Sicily and Spain. Both countries have remained under tight Catholic control ever since.

One of the positive byproducts of the Crusades was increased trade between East and West. Another was the importation into Europe of cultural advances that Muslims had made in science, mathematics, education, medicine, and philosophy. Renewed access to the works of Aristotle, rejected by the Church Fathers as "that pagan philosopher," had a major impact upon the subsequent development of Western philosophy and theology.

The tragedy of the Crusades, however, was their blatant betrayal of the law of love. Augustine may have been responsible for reversing three centuries of nonviolent church teaching and practice by unleashing the sword against the schismatic Donatists, but it would not be until the Crusades that Christians would wield the sword with such ruthless savagery. So dark is the stain of that crusading legacy that not only has Billy Graham renamed his evangelistic crusades as "missions," but some Christian universities have abandoned their "Crusader" monikers and mascots.

REFORM MOVEMENTS

The contrast could not be more striking. Seated on his throne—regaled in richly embroidered royal garments and flanked by princes of the church—sat Innocent III. Kneeling before him was a lone, barefoot monk clad only in a coarse dark robe tied at the waist with a rope. Well aware of how highly the populace regarded Francis of Assisi, the pope granted his request that the Order of Friars Minor (lesser brothers) be recognized. The pope reasoned that it would be better to keep this charismatic firebrand in the church and under his control than force him out. Thus, the Franciscan monastic movement was launched. Embracing "lady poverty," these winsome beggar-preachers turned the hearts of multitudes back to the simplicity and spirituality of New Testament Christianity. They continue to be a potent force for spirituality in the Roman Catholic Church today.

Initially renouncing education, in time the Franciscans embraced it. Oxford University became their "crown jewel." Bonaventure, Duns Scotus, and William of Occam were among their influential theologians. Franciscans, particularly in their passion for simplicity and holiness, would have a significant impact upon two 18th-century Oxford graduates: John and Charles Wesley.

Shortly before his death, Francis so mystically identified with the suffering of Christ that he is said to have received the *stigmata*, the wounds of Christ, in his own body. We remember him every time we sing his exuberant hymn of praise, "All Creatures of Our God and King."

The Dominicans were another Mendicant monastic movement established at the beginning of the 13th century. In order to gain credibility with the masses, Dominic and his followers, like the Franciscans, took vows of poverty, chastity, and obedience. They pressed the cause of Christ on three fronts. First, they sent missionaries to convert pagans in far-flung areas of the world, even penetrating the closed island-kingdom of Japan by the 17th century.

Second, they advanced learning by attaching themselves to newly established universities, such as the University of Paris, and produced some of the most influential scholars of the High Middle Ages. Among these was Thomas Aquinas.

Third, and reprehensibly, because of their passion for doctrinal orthodoxy and loyalty to the pope, they were placed in charge of Innocent III's brutal Inquisition. They bear the stigma of that cruel heritage to this day.

While the Franciscans and Dominicans were officially approved and embraced by the Church, the Cathari and the Waldenses were not. Peter Waldo gave away most of his sizeable fortune and devoted himself to a life of preaching. He attracted a large following of those who yearned to return to the simplicity and purity of the New Testament Church. They rejected oaths, war, property, veneration of saints, masses for the dead, relics, images, church taxes, indulgences, purgatory, and capital punishment. Because they regarded sacraments administered by unworthy priests as being invalid, they ordained their own clergy. While the Cathari were completely eliminated, small enclaves of the Waldenses still survive.

MYSTICS AND WOMEN

Uncomfortable with the empty rituals and worldliness of the church on the one hand, and the asceticism and legalism of the Mendicant orders on the other, many turned to mysticism in their quest for an authentic spirituality. Believing that God was beyond all being and cognitive knowing, they sought complete absorption into the Divine through prayer and contemplation. Atonement was seen not so much as an objective transaction whereby the chasm between sinful humans and a holy God was bridged, but rather as the means by which believers were progressively brought into conformity with Christ and union with God.

Thomas à Kempis (c. 1380-1471) composed what is considered to be one of the simplest and yet most profound works ever written on spirituality, *On the Imitation of Christ,* which is still read today. It was a treasured devotional companion during the critical teenage years of my own spiritual formation.

Another vitally important feature of the High Middle Ages was the strategic role of women in shaping, nurturing, and guiding the church. Though denied access to the priesthood and hierarchical ecclesial offices, they exerted enormous influence in other ways. Many, such as St. Clare, who was mightily inspired by St. Francis, founded convents where women could devote their lives to prayer, feeding the hungry, caring for the sick and elderly, and raising orphans. St. Hildegard experienced a profound religious awakening as a child. She recorded a series of visions in a widely read book, *Scivias.* She was accepted into the Benedictine order, and eventually became an abbess. She was a compelling preacher, wrote other books, traveled widely, and had an enormous impact on Emperor Fredrick Barbarossa, as well as several leaders within the church hierarchy.

LASTING LEGACY

Thanks to the rediscovery of Aristotle's works, a love of learning flourished. The Scholastics (which means "devoted to scholarship") reintroduced reason as a principle means by which the laws that govern the physical and spiritual worlds could be discovered. While revelation by definition lies beyond reason, they maintained that it is not necessarily irrational. To the contrary, the same laws of investigation, analysis, and logic that one uses to unlock the mysteries of the natural world also apply in seeking a coherent and intelligible understanding of spiritual realities.

The triumph of rationalism prepared the way for the Renaissance with its renewed appreciation for the classical cultures of Greece and Rome. Also, interest in the arts, philosophy, science, and languages blossomed. In reaction to the church's dour doctrine of original sin, these new "humanists" celebrated the infinite possibilities of realizing that which was good and beautiful in the natural world. The Renaissance, along with the Enlightenment that followed, marked a significant shift in focus from the spiritual world to the natural in all of its manifold glory. The Age of Reason opened the door for the explosive emergence of science and technology.

On the other hand, the High Middle Ages holds up a disturbing mirror of where we are today on the arc between the materialism, rationalism, and narcissistic humanism that are consuming obsessions of our times, and the poverty, simplicity, and self-giving love we see exhibited in Jesus and the apostles. The rise and fall of innumerable popes and potentates during the High Middle Ages reminds us, once again, of the futility of linking our lives and destiny to any political ideology or economic system, or of working to bring in the Kingdom through coercive juridical or legislative means.

We need to hear, with renewed attentiveness, the apostle John's warning that "all that is in the world—the desire of the flesh, the desire of the eyes, the pride in riches"—is always already passing away, "but those who do the will of God live forever" (1 John 2:16-17, NRSV). We would do well to heed the words that Jim Elliot wrote in his diary shortly before being speared by the Huaorani Indians in 1956—words that

capture the essence of the more praiseworthy spiritual im-
pulses of the High Middle Ages: "He is no fool who gives up
what he cannot keep, to gain what he cannot lose."

Notes:

1. Cited in Roland H. Bainton, *Christian Attitudes Toward War and
Peace, A Historical Survey and Critical Re-evaluation* (New York: Abingdon
Press, 1960), 115.

2. Bainton, 112-13.

Scripture Cited: Exodus 22:18; Jeremiah 48:10; 1 John 2:16-17

MARTIN LUTHER: GRIPPED BY GRACE

(15TH-16TH CENTURIES)
BY CARL M. LETH

What kind of man or woman changes history? What does it take to be a person who can impact the world for the gospel?

Martin Luther gives us a surprising—and helpful—insight into a world-changer. His background was common—no special lineage or connections. He was bright, but his genius was not in his intellect. Physically, he was unimpressive. He was thin when he was young, getting fat as he grew older. He could be deeply pious, disturbingly earthy, an engaging social partner, or a caustic critic. Emotionally, he was prone to extremes and suffered from depression that sometimes drove him to his bed. In sum, he was remarkably unexceptional. Yet, he towers in the narrative of modern history.

HIS TIME

Martin Luther was born into a time of radical and rapid change. Everywhere society was being affected by the rise of urbanization. Rapid population growth and civic expansion were making cities new centers of influence and power. Emerging centers of finance and business were moving beyond the limiting boundaries of states. The status and relationships of world powers were shifting into new configurations. Travel and trade were connecting far parts of the earth in newfound familiarity and shared (or competing) interests. New technologies made production and distribution of information widely available with surprising rapidity. The dominance of the Christian world was being challenged and threatened by the rapid expansion of an aggressive Islam. Long-dominant ways of thinking and learning were being challenged by new ideas and radically different kinds of reasoning. Even the traditional foundations of authority and the idea of Truth were being challenged. The Church was subject to spreading internal and external critique. Some proposed abandoning the church in its traditional forms altogether. The world was changing. Martin Luther lived in a world that was as unsettled as our own. His life reminds us that one person *can* make a difference.

HIS STORY

Martin Luther was born on November 10, 1483 in Eisleben, a small town in a mining region of Saxony in eastern Germany. While his family came from common stock, his father was a fairly prosperous small businessman; he operated a modest copper mine. His family was able to send him to school, enabling him to eventually earn a bachelor's degree and a master of arts degree from the University of Erfurt. In 1505, he began study with the faculty of law at the University of Erfurt. His father, like most fathers, dreamed of a better life and higher station for his son and saw the practice of law as the avenue to that goal. Martin Luther, however, struggled with the question of his vocation and his own sense of spiritual identity.

In July 1505, that struggle came to a dramatic resolution. After a visit with his family, Luther was on the road, returning to Erfurt and caught in a sudden, violent storm. A lightning strike threw him from his horse. Frightened and confronted by the reality of his mortality, he cried out to St. Anne, the patron saint of miners and people in distress in thunderstorms, promising to become a monk if she aided him. This experience resolved his personal crisis. Abandoning his pursuit of the legal profession (despite his father's disapproval), he entered the Augustinian monastery of Erfurt.

Luther's vocational uncertainties were settled by his admission to the monastery, but his personal spiritual struggle was only beginning. The monastic life practiced at Erfurt called him to live a life of holiness before God. Luther undertook that challenge with energy and commitment. He also brought an exceptionally sensitive conscience.

For Luther, monastic life was an exercise in rigor and human effort to be worthy of God's grace. In his frequent times of confession, he would review in extended detail his faults—what he did or didn't do, his wrong or unworthy attitudes, his excessive pride over his humility, and his excessive humility that might become pride. As soon as he would complete a lengthy confession, he would be troubled that he had not been contrite enough or that he was taking inappropriate comfort in the earnestness of his contrition. He drove his confessor to distraction, who at one point urged Luther to come back after he had committed some "real sins." Yet no matter how rigorous his attempts to be holy, he always fell short. His pursuit of holiness was an ongoing exercise in frustration.

In 1511, Luther was sent to the University of Wittenberg, where he earned his doctorate in theology and remained as professor of Bible. In the course of his extended lectures on the Psalms, Galatians, and Romans, Luther experienced a spiritual breakthrough that would not only transform his life, but would shape the coming Reformation. Luther's was a leap forward in his understanding of God's righteousness. The demands of God's justice, which Luther could never satisfy, were met by God himself in Christ. It is not our works of righteousness that God desires, but our faith in Christ, whose righteousness justifies us before God. We are not justified before God by *our* works but by God's grace *alone,* through faith in Christ and His promise of mercy. Luther experienced the liberation of grace from the burden of self-justification. *Justification by grace through faith* became the focus of Luther's personal reformation and the "gospel" of the Reformation he would lead.

While Luther had been discovering the liberation of God's grace on his behalf, he was also becoming increasingly concerned with the state of the church and the message of "easy" grace dispensed by the church. The Roman church entering the 16th century was wealthy and powerful and not always spiritual in its leadership. It often looked—and acted—like a secular empire. Yet, it was also subject to repeated attempts at reform. Many church leaders were unhappy with the abuses and campaigned for reform. Nonetheless, there was a widespread impression that the church was corrupt and self-absorbed, disconnected from the common person and real spiritual life.

The church had developed the doctrine of a "treasury of merit" that was at the disposal of the church. In a positive sense, it expressed the important role of the church as a means, or channel, of God's grace. However, that doctrine had become the source of significant abuse, making the benefits of the treasury available for purchase. In principle, the benefits were linked to genuine contrition of the heart, expressed in the offering given. In practice, the benefits were understood to be simply available for the purchase price.

Entrepreneurial churchmen were not slow to develop money-raising schemes. Luther's region became the "market" for an aggressive salesman for indulgences, the official granting of grace. Especially compelling was the argument that you could shorten the time a loved one had to spend in purgatory before going on to heaven. What loving son could refuse to shorten a deceased parent's suffering if it was in his power to do so? The indulgence salesman even had a marketing jingle. "When a coin in the coffer clings, a soul from purgatory heavenward springs."

In 1517, Martin Luther posted his 95 theses on the door of the castle church in Wittenberg. His theses were presented in Latin and in a form intended to prompt theological discussion among academics and church leaders. Nevertheless, they were soon translated and became a matter of public debate and controversy. Luther had "accidentally" stumbled into the Reformation.

The public controversy escalated through repeated public debates and published exchanges until the pope condemned Luther's writings in 1520 in a formal declaration (a papal "bull"). Luther had 60 days to recant. Facing condemnation and excommunication by the recognized leader of the church, Luther refused to back down.

In 1521, the assembled leaders of the Holy Roman Empire gathered in Worms (pronounced "Vorms") to meet with the emperor in an official meeting called a "Diet" (a kind of legislative body). Luther was called to face the members of the Diet and accused of condemned teachings. When his recantation was demanded, he asked for a day to consider his response. His position was precarious. Even though he had been promised safe passage to and from the Diet, a declared heretic could not depend on that promise. The troops of the sympathetic Baron Franz von Sickingen were nearby, but there was no assurance that their assistance would be enough. To refuse the demand of the Diet to recant might well mean death by burning at the stake. Was his belief in the gospel of salvation by grace through faith worth his life?

The next day, Luther stood before the assembled leaders of most of Europe, facing the emperor of the Holy Roman Empire. The gist of his reply is captured in the declaration, "Here I stand. I can do no other. God help me." There was no turning back.

It merits mentioning that Luther's courage was not merely the product of a bold personality. In fact, Luther was plagued throughout his life with personal doubts and periods of depression. His courage at Worms—and throughout his career—should be seen as the product of a radical obedience to God and a willingness to trust God despite the consequences, even when God could not be clearly seen or felt. That is, after all, the most profound kind of courage.

Luther lived a long life for his era. He outlived most of his contemporaries and shouldered the heavy responsibilities of leading the Reformation. Constantly under attack and often suffering from painful physical ailments, he paid a steep price for his commitment to reformation. In 1546, old, sick, and weary, he made one more trip—from Wittenberg to Eisleben to mediate a dispute between the Counts of Mansfeld. There, just down the street from where he had been born, Martin Luther died, affirming in his deathbed testimony his abiding commitment to the gospel he had taught.

THE PRINCIPLES AT STAKE

Luther confronted two different messages about grace. Both attempted to respond to the question, "How do we find an assurance of God's grace in the face of His righteousness?" Neither answered that question in a way that resolved Luther's personal struggle of faith.

One answer was represented by the sale of indulgences. It was grace without price. Even in the church's understanding of the sacraments, grace was conveyed with little expectation of the recipient. Grace was given if the sacrament was rightly celebrated by a properly ordained priest. As long as a recipient did not consciously reject the grace, it was conveyed. This is one reason the Latin mass could be celebrated by people who did not understand Latin. They didn't need to understand. They simply needed to be willing to receive grace (or at least be unopposed to receiving grace). The benefit was that recipients could be reasonably certain that grace was effective for them, but this reduced the merit of Christ's death to a commodity to be dispensed.

While we no longer sell indulgences, it is worth considering our understanding of God's grace and how it works. Some would hold that our participation in the liturgy or worship service is enough for God's grace to save us. If we are a willing part of the community of the church, that should be enough for God's grace to work. If the church is holy, and we are participating in the life of the church, aren't we holy too? If we go to church and pay our tithe, shouldn't that be enough?

The other answer was our contribution to our own justification. If we do what we are able to, then God will do the rest. God's grace "finishes" our justification, but we "begin" it. Still, how can we be sure that we have done what we can do? In fact, doesn't the problem of sin guarantee that we will never be able to really meet that standard?

The problem of double justification did not end with the 16th century. While we affirm God's grace as necessary and available for our salvation, we also often hear that we must do what we can do first. We must work as far as we can go before God's grace takes over. Salvation becomes a team project—except that our half of the team isn't up to the challenge.

Caught between the illusion of cheap grace and the bondage of earning grace, Martin Luther discovered the message of God's gift of grace that saves us by faith in Him. It is free—when we place our faith in Christ. We cannot earn it. In fact, God wants us to surrender trying to show that we deserve it. And while it is free, it is not casually or accidentally given. We are saved by grace through faith—in Christ. "We are all beggars," Luther once wrote, adding in the margin, "This is true." But we are all beggars for whom Christ died and for whom His grace applies.

> Did we in our own strength confide,
> Our striving would be losing;
> Were not the right Man on our side,
> The Man of God's own choosing.
> Dost ask who that may be?
> Christ Jesus—it is He; . . .
> And He must win the battle.
> ("A Mighty Fortress Is Our God," Martin Luther, 1529)

It is an irony that Martin Luther was actually more afraid of God than the devil. The devil's evil was frightening, but the prospect of facing God in His holiness and unrestrained power was far more terrifying. How can a person find peace and assurance despite his or her own unworthiness before such an all-powerful and holy God? Luther found his answer in trusting in the promise of a God who died on a cross for him.

THE REST OF THE STORY

Martin Luther's impact continues to be felt today. Most people would be hard-pressed to name the powerful leaders who opposed and threatened him. Yet, they remember the common man of uncommon courage and conviction who helped change their world.

Luther's "rediscovery" of the doctrine of justification by grace through faith and his unrelenting call to its central importance for the gospel is probably his most significant legacy. It continues to be a central tenet of Christian faith—including the modern Roman Catholic Church. It still needs to be balanced by the call of the gospel to transformation of heart and life. We are justified by grace, but we are justified to be *changed* by grace. Inheritors of Luther have sometimes emphasized the doctrine of justification by grace so strongly that the complementary message of transformation by that grace—holiness —has been overlooked or forgotten. Nevertheless, it is important to remember that we are not made holy to *earn* our salvation. We are justified by grace—alone—though faith.

Martin Luther can also serve us as an example of a life lived in obedience to God in a critical time in human history. In most ways, Luther was not so different from most of us. In a sense, his life echoes his discovery of justification by grace through faith. It wasn't his ability or achievements that God needed to redirect a world in transition. It was Luther's trusting obedience (that could become obstinate courage) that God needed. Martin Luther gave that obedience to God—and changed history.

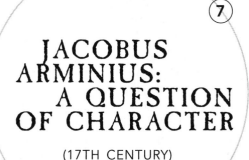

JACOBUS ARMINIUS: A QUESTION OF CHARACTER

(17TH CENTURY)
CARL M. LETH

Times of reformation and renewal are often followed by times of extremes. Opposition to formalism becomes a new formalism. Correctives to excesses in doctrine and practice become excessive in another direction. Inspired messages become the basis for new rigid rules.

In those times, the most uncomfortable place to be is the center. The most unwelcome message is a call for balance or moderation. The most provocative personality is a gentle spirit.

Jacobus Arminius was a man born into just such a time. The Reformation that Martin Luther inaugurated in 1517 divided Europe. Conflict between the Protestants and Roman Catholics was echoed in heightening conflict between different Protestant parties. Any spirit of moderation was seen as unacceptable compromise. An unlikely candidate for controversy, Arminius became the center of a national conflict, but what he had to say continues to influence our history.

BEGINNINGS*

Jacobus Arminius was born in 1559 in Oudewater, Holland. He was very young when his father died (perhaps even before his birth). A fairly successful tradesman (perhaps as

61

an armorer), his death left his wife and young children in difficult, but not desperate, straits. It is possible that the family business was kept in operation and a network of relations provided assistance and support. These relatives helped young Arminius in 1574 or early 1575 to make his way to study at the University of Marburg, a young, Protestant university founded by Phillip of Marburg (Hesse) in 1527.

Outside the quiet community of Oudewater, conflict was building. The influence of the Reformation was challenging the dominance of the Roman Catholic Church. In the Netherlands, that religious struggle had produced military conflict. Protestant and Catholic forces fought back and forth across the region. Although Oudewater was Catholic when Arminius was born, it became Protestant in 1574. In 1575, Spanish Catholic troops attacked the town, resulting in a near-total massacre of the inhabitants, including Arminius's mother and siblings.

Devastated by this loss, Arminius abandoned his plans to study at Marburg and returned home to Holland. In 1576, he became the 12th student to enter the University of Leiden. It had been founded in 1575 to provide Dutch students a Protestant university. There, he began to establish the foundations of his theological thought. A key foundation was a de-emphasis on speculative or theoretical theology. Theology should be practical in its concerns. It serves the life of the Church. The object of theology is to incline us to worship God and to persuade us to that practice. Arminius's practice of theology throughout his life reflected this commitment.

By 1581, Arminius had completed his studies at Leiden. The Merchant's Guild in Amsterdam approved a financial subsidy for his further theological studies, with his commitment to return and serve as a pastor in Amsterdam. This support enabled his travel to Switzerland to study in Geneva and Basel, centers of the Reformed movement.

In Geneva, he studied under Theodore Beza, the successor of John Calvin. Beza, however, was more rigid in his theology than his mentor. Calvin affirmed God's sovereignty and providence as a starting point for theology. The doctrine of predestination was an aspect of his thought, but never a central principle. It belonged more properly to the mysteries of God—something we should believe but not try to fully understand or reconcile with human reasoning. For Beza, predestination became a central doctrine, embedded in rigorous reasoning that shaped the rest of his understanding of God and salvation. In this period of his education, Arminius wrestled with the ideas that would eventually define his ministry and his legacy.

Finished with his studies in Switzerland, Arminius finally returned to Amsterdam in 1587. After a process of examination, he was approved to begin his pastoral work. In 1588, he began 15 years of pastoral ministry in Amsterdam. In September 1590, he married Lijsbet Reael, daughter of a successful and influential businessman in Amsterdam. In 1591 and 1592, their first two children were born and died in infancy. Though Arminius's writings reveal very few of Arminius's feelings, these must have been difficult days for the young pastor and his young wife. In 1593, their daughter Angelica was born—and survived. In all, Jacob and Lijsbet had 12 children, 9 of whom survived infancy. Lijsbet would live a long life, surviving her husband and all but two of her children.

From the beginning, there were suggestions of the struggle to come. As early as 1520, a reformation party had been active in Holland. By the end of the 16th century, Protestant Holland was divided between those sharing an earlier reformation understanding—with a more moderate view of providence and election—and the more rigorous predestination of Beza and his followers. This difference would sharpen into lines of division and open conflict. In 1592 and again in 1593, complaints were lodged against Arminius by this more rigorous party concerning his views on predestination. In both cases, the charges were reviewed and rejected.

At the end of the 16th century, Amsterdam was entering its golden era. From a role as a minor center of trade, Amsterdam was becoming a world center. The famous Dutch East Indies Company was formed. This eventually had significant implications for Arminius. Some of his key opponents were associated with the company. Petrus Plancius, a prominent pastor in Amsterdam and determined critic of Arminius, was a prominent partner in the company. As its success and political power grew, the balance of political support for Arminius's moderate views shifted. Traditional leaders—who were sympathetic to the older, moderate party—were supplanted by new, more rigorous leaders. In the end, the success of trade and sailing ships would play an important role in affecting the theology of a nation.

In the midst of these emerging changes, Arminius served as a pastor. He preached, taught, visited, and shared the life of his parishioners. In 1601, the plague struck Amsterdam, with devastating effect. Some 20,000 died, at a rate of as many as 1,000 a day. Arminius served faithfully in the city throughout the plague and was praised for his ministry. It is significant to note that his later theological writings as a professor of theology were a product of his development as a pastor. This perspective shaped how Arminius approached the task of theology and his understanding of its purpose.

A QUESTION OF GRACE

The issues that continued to swirl around Arminius throughout his life became increasingly clear in this pastoral period. They centered on God's character, revealed in election, the question of the free will of humans, and the understanding of the role of God's grace.

Theodore Beza and the more rigorous reformed party that followed him had radicalized Calvin's reformation theology. Beginning with a resolute emphasis on God's sovereignty and absolute providence, God's work of salvation became a logical conclusion rather than a dynamic mystery. God was in control. He directed history. Even the Fall became a part of the plan. Humans had been placed in a situation where it was certain that they would sin—in fact, they could not do otherwise. Nevertheless, humans had willingly (if necessarily) sinned and were therefore guilty, thus earning judgment and eternal punishment.

God had acted in Christ to save, but salvation was determined by God alone. The atoning work of Christ was not for everyone. It was really only for the elect, those whom God had chosen. When the offer of salvation was proclaimed, only those elected would really hear it, prompted to respond by God's grace that moved them. That saving grace (which moves us to repentance and faith) is selectively given. Only those who are given that grace will be saved.

While these ideas had been discussed by the Church since Augustine in the 4th century, the 16th- and 17th-century Dutch Calvinists gave them a new emphasis and rigorous interpretation. They became, for them, the central issues of the Reformation.

Arminius, however, rejected the idea that God had a revealed will and a (different) secret will. Would God reveal a general invitation to salvation ("Come to me, all you who are weary and burdened, and I will give you rest" [Matthew 11:28]) that His secret will did not intend (since only the elect would actually be saved)? Arminius held that God's call was a "serious" call. God intended what He said. Those who *are* invited *may* come.

This had implications for his understanding of human free will and the role of God's grace. For Arminius, the free will of fallen humanity is unable to choose the good. It is captive to the power of sin. Our salvation is totally dependent upon the gift of God's grace to help us. Unless God acts to save us, we will certainly be lost. Thankfully, God has acted in Christ to save us, but this gift of God's grace does not, therefore, force us to choose the good. Rather, *God's grace enables our ability to freely choose God, but does not coerce it.* Our salvation is, in this sense, totally dependent upon God's grace, but effectively limited by our will. We may choose *not* to respond to God positively.

At issue is the matter of God's character. First of all, it concerns the question of God's integrity. Is God a God who deceives? Would He proclaim an offer of grace that He did not really give? Would He act as if anyone may come when He meant anyone *He chooses* may come? Are human beings real dialogue partners with God or simply puppets moved by God's direction? Is the drama of salvation history simply a pre-scripted play that God orchestrates by himself?

Second, is God's character determined by His sovereignty alone? Or is His exercise of sovereignty determined by His character of love? Can human logic adequately explain the mystery of salvation? Isn't the atonement of Christ a mystery of love rather than the conclusion of human logic?

Arminius defended the integrity of God in His revelation. God calls to all because it is possible for all of us to answer. God calls because it is possible for us *not* to answer. The conclusion is not determined apart from our response. The drama of salvation that reveals a seeking, inviting God is real. The character of God's love moves the story and directs His providence. Grace is not merely a force, it is a Person—the Holy Spirit. Because it is a Person, grace will not coerce our relationship with Him.

THE FINAL CHAPTER

By 1603, Arminius's reputation was well established. The high regard of his contemporaries for Arminius as a theologian prompted the invitation to return to the University of Leiden as a professor of theology. Reluctantly, Arminius left his pastoral assignment and assumed his new responsibilities in Leiden. Before he began teaching, he was granted the doctor in theology from the University of Leiden, only the second doctorate to be awarded by the university. At the age of 44, he was at his peak —active and vigorous. But he was also troubled by persistent "colds" (probably early stages of tuberculosis) that would become more troublesome for him during the remaining six years of his life.

Almost from the beginning, theological tensions heightened. Public and written debate increased in intensity, becoming a focal point of national debate. In October 1604, Franciscus Gomarus, a fellow professor of theology, offered a public disagreement that took sharp exception to Arminius's views. The central issue was election and predestination. Arminius taught that God's predestination concerned the plan of salvation. God predestined salvation for those who believed and judgment to those who would not believe. Gomarus insisted that predestination was individual and foreordained. God moved some individually to belief and salvation, while relegating others individually to damnation. God alone determined who would be saved and who would be damned.

Despite the controversy, Arminius was elected as the chief officer of the university in 1605, indicating the respect of his fellow faculty. He completed his tenure (it was a one-year term) in 1606 with a closing speech: "On Reconciling Religious Dissensions Among Christians." In this speech, he lamented the destructive character of dissension and conflict between Christians. It was a plea for tolerance that fell on deaf ears. The debate continued with increasing vigor. In 1608, Arminius and his chief opponent, Gomarus, were called before the High Council of the States of Holland in an attempt to resolve the increasingly divisive conflict. They were directed to prepare formal statements to be submitted to the council.

Arminius would not, however, be able to see this debate through to its completion. The signs of illness he had shown as early as 1603 had become persistent and more pronounced. Throughout much of the controversy with Gomarus, he had been seriously ill. The strain of the controver-

sy probably contributed to his declining health. His illness
grew increasingly severe, finally taking his life on October
19, 1609.

After Arminius's death, more than 40 pastors signed a
document called the Remonstrance of 1610, which affirmed
the positions he had advocated. Years of heightened conflict
continued until opponents of Arminius were able to forcibly
remove the "Remonstrants" from power. In 1618-19, a national synod was convened at Dort which refused to recognize any Remonstrant delegates, seating only their opponents. Not surprisingly, their views—and the positions of
Arminius—were condemned.

LEGACY

The condemnation by the Synod of Dort would not,
however, be the end of the story. This national council and
its judgments never achieved recognition beyond the theological party that controlled it. Arminius—and those who
shared his views—would continue to have influence on the
life of the Church. John Wesley was a prominent inheritor of
"Arminianism" (which is why our tradition is sometimes referred to as Wesleyan-Arminian). Even beyond the tradition
that identifies explicitly with Arminius, the history of the
Church has largely validated his views, and even Reformed
traditions are influenced today by his legacy.

In addition to his theological positions, Arminius serves
as an example for the practice of theology. While clearly
competent as a technical theologian, he always understood
theology to be primarily a practical discipline. His pastoral
orientation focused his theological interests on matters per-
taining to salvation and understanding God's character and
will concerning salvation. This practical approach to theology would also be followed by John Wesley and the tradition
that followed him.

Arminius also leaves us an example of moderation in a

time of extremes. His writings are never very personal and reveal little of his feelings. Still, his behavior and response to those who criticized him demonstrated grace and moderation and a persistent attempt to find resolution. He was firm in his views, but gracious in his manner.

A QUESTION OF CHARACTER

Arminius's vision of God affirmed His sovereignty without denying the critical role of human response. It affirmed the priority—and necessity—of God's grace without determining human response. He affirmed the truth and importance of God's drama of salvation that seeks a lost and rebellious humanity, calling us to "come home." Our salvation is all by God's grace, but God's grace will not save us without us. It was here that Arminius, who was always a pastoral theologian, saw the heart of the gospel.

*This account of Arminius's life and ministry relies on the standard work by Carl Bangs, *Arminius: A Study in the Dutch Reformation* (Nashville: Abingdon, 1971).

Scripture Cited: Matthew 11:28

JOHN AND CHARLES WESLEY: LOVE AFLAME

(18TH CENTURY)
BY C. S. COWLES

While the mighty English navy and red-coated army were seizing great chunks of the world's real estate for the Crown under the guise of bringing Christianity and civilization to pagan peoples, their own homeland was being savaged by the Industrial Revolution. The move from an agrarian to manufacturing economy precipitated a flood of landless peasants pouring into the cities, bringing in its wake massive social dislocation, grinding poverty, and increasing lawlessness. Smoke-spewing factories were able to churn out armaments and manufactured goods, making the British Empire the richest and most powerful nation of the 18th century, only by consuming the bodies and souls of the poor. Orphans disappeared into the coal mines, never to see the light of day again. Children as young as six were forced by beatings and starvation to slave alongside adults 14 hours a day in textile factories. Workers lucky enough to find shelter often shared their squalid rooms with a dozen others. Horse manure piled up 14 feet high on London's streets!

The government responded to the rising tide of crime, fueled by economic deprivation and spiritual dislocation, by making over 200 offenses punishable by death. One could be hung for stealing a loaf of bread. The judicial system became an inhumane machine that devoured the disadvantaged through executions and deportation to the convict colony of Australia. Plagues of typhoid, smallpox, dysentery, and cholera cut like a scythe through densely populated ghettos. As the gap between the impoverished masses and powerful elite grew greater, the accumulation of outrages raised the social temperature to a flash point that threatened to consume the nation in a fury of self-destruction like that which occurred in France across the English Channel.

THE FLAME THAT CHANGED THE WORLD

The wildfire that swept across England, however, was not that of a violent social revolution whose terrifying symbol was the ubiquitous guillotine, as in France, but rather the holy flame of one of the most transformative spiritual revivals in history. The spark that touched it off was struck on May 24, 1738, in the most unlikely of places—a Moravian Bible study; and in the heart of a most unremarkable person —a frustrated Anglican priest. John Wesley (1703-1791) wrote of that epic event:

> In the evening I went very unwillingly to a society in Aldersgate Street, where one was reading Luther's preface to the Epistle to the Romans. About a quarter before nine, while he was describing the change which God works in the heart through faith in Christ, I felt my heart strangely warmed. I felt I did trust in Christ, Christ alone for salvation: And an assurance was given me, that he had taken away *my* sins, even *mine,* and saved *me* from the law of sin and death.[1]

Wesley's "strangely warmed" heart precipitated the great Evangelical Awakening that not only changed the hearts and lives of tens of thousands, but generated far-reaching social reforms. Wesley, and the Methodist movement that emerged under his leadership, worked to abolish child labor, agitated to make working conditions more humane, sought to reform the judicial system and penal institutions, and abolish slavery. He championed equal rights for women, encouraged the emerging labor movement, instituted social welfare programs, founded the first credit union so that the poor could help themselves, established rescue missions and homes for unwed mothers, and organized schools for all ages. Not only did the Wesleyan revival go a long way toward cleansing the rot that was eating away at the soul of the Empire, but it leaped the Atlantic to become a powerful force in the shaping of America's emerging national character.

Wesley's blend of experiential religion and social responsibility was ingenious. The *Gentleman's Magazine,* that had repeatedly blasted Wesley during his lifetime, published this tribute following his death on March 2, 1791:

> It is impossible to deny him the merit of having done infinite good to the lower classes of people. . . . By the humane endeavors of him and his brother, Charles, a sense of decency in morals and religion was introduced in the lowest classes of mankind, the ignorant were instructed, and the wretched relieved and the abandoned reclaimed. . . . He must be considered as one of the most extraordinary characters this or any other age has ever produced.

FORMATIVE YEARS

John was the 15th and Charles the 18th of 19 children born to Samuel Wesley, an Anglican priest, and his wife, Susanna. Eight died in infancy. John often described himself, after being rescued from a fire that consumed the rectory, as "a brand plucked out of the burning."[2] From his mother, he received both his early education and a passion for the things of God.

While attending Oxford University, John and Charles led a small group of students called the "Holy Club." Because of the methodical manner in which they devoted themselves to Bible reading, prayer, fasting, almsgiving, Holy

Communion, visitation of prisoners, and mutual accountability, they were derisively called "Methodists." The name
stuck.

After John was ordained an Anglican priest, he and
Charles volunteered for missionary service to the American
colonies. He applied himself with uncommon zeal to his
labors in Georgia. He demonstrated remarkable linguistic
abilities by conducting worship services in German, French,
and Italian, as well as English. Yet, his intense manner and
severe spirit alienated people. After two years and a failed
romance, he left in frustration and defeat.

During a ferocious storm at sea, the Wesley brothers
could not help but be impressed by the cheerful courage of
26 Moravians, who possessed an assurance of salvation that
the Wesleys did not have. Shortly after returning home, they
sought out Peter Bohler, a Moravian, who convinced them
concerning instantaneous conversion, complete self-surren-
der in faith, and joy in believing. While in the grip of a serious illness, Charles underwent a heartfelt conversion on May
21, 1738. His brother's spiritual awakening followed three
days later.

A MOVEMENT TAKES SHAPE

Like Saul of Tarsus following his Damascus road encounter with the living Christ, "something like scales fell
from [his] eyes" (Acts 9:18), and John Wesley immediately
began to proclaim the "amazing grace" of Jesus Christ far
and wide. For people long oppressed by the tyranny of An-
glo-catholic works-salvation on the one hand and trapped in
John Calvin's doctrine of individual predestination on the
other, Wesley's fervent preaching took the nation by storm.
Though Calvin's intention had been to ground believer's
faith on the solid rock of God's absolute sovereignty, it had
the opposite effect; that is, how were they to know if they
were among the "elect"? Instead of "eternal security," people

were terrorized by "anxious insecurity." Wesley himself had formerly been tormented by worry over his salvation.

Not so following Aldersgate. No text thereafter was more often upon his lips than that "the Spirit himself testifies with our spirit that we are God's children" (Romans 8:16). He described assurance as "an inward impression on the soul, whereby the Spirit of God directly witnesses to my spirit, that I am a child of God; that Jesus Christ has loved me, and given himself for me; and that all my sins are blotted out, and I, even I, am reconciled to God."[3]

Over against the despair precipitated by a deeply entrenched Calvinistic theology that wrote off the poor and wretched masses as not being among the "elect elite"—and thus irrevocably doomed—Wesley proclaimed the "good news" that "everyone who calls on the name of the Lord will be saved" (Romans 10:13). On a historic Sunday morning, April 29, 1739, he stood before an open-air crowd of 4,000 and delivered a sermon that may be fairly claimed to have launched England's Great Evangelical Awakening. "How freely does God love the world," he exulted. "While we were yet sinners, 'Christ died for the ungodly.' While we were 'dead in sin,' God 'spared not his own Son, but delivered him up for us all.' And how freely does he 'give us all things!' Verily, Free Grace is all in all!"[4]

It is no wonder that such preaching elicited an enthusiastic response. The poor and disenfranchised began to believe that they were loved and accepted by God, and that they could improve themselves and their lot in life. And that is exactly what they did. Our world is still reaping the benefits of the dynamic spiritual forces unleashed and social reforms initiated.

THE LIBERATING GOSPEL OF HEART HOLINESS

Wesley proclaimed a salvation that not only changed

one's status before God, as held by Luther and Calvin, but that radically transformed one's heart and life. He taught that believers could experience, in this life, the joy of a clean heart filled with nothing but love for God and for all peoples.

Anglican liturgy included this petition in the Communion service:

> Almighty God, unto whom all hearts are open, all desires known, and from whom no secrets are hid: Cleanse the thoughts of our hearts by the inspiration of thy Holy Spirit, that we may perfectly love thee, and worthily magnify thy holy Name, through Christ our Lord. *Amen.*

Wesley frequently quoted this prayer, known to every Anglican by heart, because it captured the essence of his doctrine of entire sanctification. Tragically, even though people prayed it every time they partook of Holy Communion, the idea that their prayers could be answered in their lifetimes seemed incredulous.

Yet, Wesley fearlessly preached that Christ's atoning work on the Cross avails not only for the forgiveness of sins, but for the cleansing of the heart from the inherited nature of sin. Believers could, by faith, enter into a present-tense sanctifying experience of a heart full of nothing but love for God and for the neighbor. The gospel offers more than freedom from the guilt of sin; "it is the power of God for the salvation [from all sin] of everyone who believes" (Romans 1:16). A sanctified believer is not exempt from *temptations* to sin or the *possibility* of sin, but delivered from the *compulsion* to sin. The one who has been "freed from sin" can enjoy a continuous relationship of complete devotion to God, "resulting in sanctification, and the outcome, eternal life" (Romans 6:22, NASB).

It was this "holy optimism" in regard to the experience and practice of heart holiness that represented Wesley's greatest contribution to Christian theology. Not only has entire sanctification become the defining doctrine of the Wes-

leyan movement, but it has been the driving force behind today's emphasis upon the Spirit-filled life of total commitment to Christ found among evangelicals everywhere.

MANY ARENAS OF MINISTRY

Wesley was known as the busiest man in England. He
traveled over 250,000 miles on horseback, traversed the
British Isles many times preaching, teaching, forming societies, opening chapels, examining and commissioning
preachers, administering discipline, raising funds for the
poor, visiting prisoners, praying for the sick, superintending
schools and orphanages, and conversing at length with
friends and foes. He translated the entire New Testament
from Greek into English, mostly while riding on his horse.
He wrote and edited more than 200 books, commentaries,
hymnbooks, and pamphlets. He published an English grammar, a medical manual that became a runaway bestseller, a
dictionary, and textbooks. He pressed for the abolition of
slavery, the end of child labor, the cause of peace, and justice
for the poor. He kept a daily diary, as well as a journal. And
he carried on a copious correspondence, much of which has
been preserved. Wesley's written works comprise a Christian
library in excess of 50 volumes.

INNOVATIONS

Though Wesley was deeply committed to the doctrines
and practices of the Anglican church, the practical necessi-
ties generated by the growing revival made innovation a necessity. High-church liturgy gave way to simplicity in worship. Instead of a clergy-dominated ministry, he encouraged
lay participation and leadership. Lecture-style preaching
yielded to speaking "plain truth for plain people" in plain
language.[5]

Methodist meetings were notorious for their spirited
singing of hymns, written in the idiom of the common peo-

ple. Charles, a gifted poet and musician, made a contribution of epic proportions to Methodist worship. He became the most prolific hymn writer in history, with over 6,600 hymns to his credit, some having as many as 18 verses.

Converts began to multiply. Since these new believers came, for the most part, from the lowest classes, they were not welcome in Anglican churches. So, Wesley formed them into small groups in order to pray together, receive the word of exhortation, and watch over one another in love. What began out of necessity in order to nurture those without a church home morphed into an organization designed to conserve and multiply the fruits of the revival. Each Methodist society was subdivided into class meetings of about a dozen people, led by lay leaders. At the time, they were the only democratic forums in England. They welcomed into their embrace rich and poor, learned and illiterate, men *and* women. Their effectiveness in spiritual formation can be seen in that nearly 40 percent of active evangelical Christians today are involved in some sort of small prayer and Bible study group. This is one of Wesley's many enduring legacies.

Another tradition-breaking and far-reaching innovation was the significant role that women played in the Wesleyan revival. When Wesley saw how God was pleased to call and use gifted women in evangelism and spiritual nurture (some preached to crowds numbered in the thousands), he overcame his inherited Anglican bias against women preachers. He commissioned them to preach, and appointed those who had special aptitudes to leadership positions in his societies and class meetings.

THE CATHOLIC SPIRIT

John and Charles Wesley were lifelong Anglicans. Though often banned from its pulpits and harassed by its clergy, they never ceased to love the church and work for its welfare. It was never their intention to form a new denomination. To the contrary, they regarded their societies as extensions of the established church. It was only after decades of unremitting rejection by the ecclesiastical establishment that Methodism began to consider itself a separate movement, raised up by God to "spread scriptural holiness."[6] Yet, the Wesley brothers themselves died as they had lived— faithful Anglicans.

Wesley abhorred provincialism and sectarianism in any form. He pled, "If we cannot as yet think alike in all things, at least we may love alike."[7] Wesley affirmed, "'If thine heart is as my heart,' if thou lovest God and all mankind, I ask no more: 'Give me thine hand.'"[8] One of the present denominations which traces its roots back to Methodism succinctly captures Wesley's ecumenical spirit: "The Church of God is composed of all spiritually regenerate persons, whose names are written in heaven."[9]

John Wesley died on March 2, 1791. At the time of his death, the growing Methodist movement was 135,000 members strong, and was served by 541 itinerant (traveling) preachers. It has since grown to include nearly 100 Wesleyan denominations worldwide. The impact of Wesley's life, the ecclesial innovations and social reforms he set in motion, and the transformative influence of his theology reaches far beyond those churches that consider themselves Wesleyan. It is with good reason that Wesley is regarded as one of the half-dozen most influential personalities in Protestant Christianity.

Wesley's life, ministry, and theology are best summed up in the answer he gave to the question, "What is the essence of the sanctified life?" His response is not only eloquent in its own right, but goes to the very heart of the glorious gospel of Christ:

> It were well you should be thoroughly sensible of this, —"the heaven of heavens is love." There is nothing higher in religion; there is, in effect, nothing else; if you look for anything but more love, you are looking wide of

the mark, you are getting out of the royal way. And when you are asking others, "Have you received this or that blessing?" if you mean anything but more love, you mean wrong; you are leading them out of the way, and putting them upon a false scent. Settle it then in your heart, that from the moment God has saved you from all sin, you are to aim at nothing more, but more of that love described in the thirteenth of the Corinthians. You can go no higher than this, till you are carried into Abraham's bosom.[10]

Notes:

1. "Journals 1735-1745," *The Complete Works of John Wesley*, vol. 1 (Albany, Oreg.: AGES Software, 1997), 124.

2. "Letters and Writings," *Works*, vol. 13, 491.

3. "The Witness of the Spirit," *Works*, vol. 5, 187.

4. "Free Grace," *Works*, vol. 7, 416.

5. "Preface," *Works*, vol. 5, 66.

6. "Minutes of Several Conversations," *Works*, vol. 8, 346.

7. "A Letter to a Roman Catholic," *Works*, vol. 10, 104.

8. "Catholic Spirit," *Works*, vol. 5, 603.

9. *Manual Church of the Nazarene 2005-2009* (Kansas City: Nazarene Publishing House, 2005), 39.

10. "A Plain Account of Christian Perfection," *Works*, vol. 11, 504.

Scripture Cited: Acts 9:18; Romans 1:16; 6:22; 8:16; 10:13

FRANCIS ASBURY: AN OFFER OF MYSELF

(18TH-19TH CENTURIES)
BY FLOYD CUNNINGHAM

On August 7, 1771, the Methodist Conference, meeting in Bristol, England, resolved to send two additional preachers to America. Quickly 25-year-old Francis Asbury, an itinerant preacher, "spoke his mind," as he wrote in his *Journal*, and "made an offer of myself."[1] John Wesley accepted the offer and appointed Asbury to the American circuit. Throughout his long, rugged life, Asbury never wavered from this appointment, and never withdrew his "offer" of himself.

Methodism had already spread to America through Methodist immigrants from Ireland. About 1760, unknown to each other, Irish lay preachers Robert Strawbridge settled in Maryland, and Phillip Embury in New York. Until the American Revolution, Methodists cooperated with the Church of England, yet also erected meetinghouses of their own. In 1769, Wesley sent his first official representatives.

BECOMING A METHODIST

Unlike John and Charles Wesley, sons of a priest of the Church of England and graduates of Oxford University, Francis Asbury was from a common family and had little formal education. Asbury was born in Handsworth, Staffordshire, England, August 20 or 21, 1745, the only surviving child of Joseph and Elizabeth Rogers Asbury. The death of an infant daughter (Asbury's sister) led to his mother's conversion. Asbury's father was a farmer and gardener. He apprenticed his son to a local blacksmith, who happened to be a Methodist.

Asbury, a devout and studious child, was spiritually "awakened" before the age of 14. He read some sermons of George Whitefield, and, with friends, attended a Methodist meeting a few miles from his home. He felt himself under conviction. Afterward, when praying in his father's barn, he believed the Lord pardoned his sins. Yet under the influence of others, Asbury lost his confidence in the experience. Some months later, he realized that he had indeed the assurance of his salvation that the Methodists discussed.

Asbury began holding prayer meetings in his father's house, and through his exhortations, several souls professed to find peace. By age 18, he was a licensed preacher. At 21, Asbury became a full-time itinerant in the Methodist connection. For the next years, he made his way around various circuits, preaching up to five times a week.

A few weeks after the 1771 Conference, Asbury bid tearful farewell to his father and mother, and boarded a ship to America. When he departed from England, it was never to return. More than any other preacher sent to America by Wesley, Asbury identified himself with the American people.

PREACHING IN AMERICA

Upon arriving, Asbury immediately assessed the situation in America by traveling to Methodist societies and meetinghouses from north to south. As Asbury itinerated throughout the colonies, he felt burdened with the overwhelming spiritual needs of the people. Methodists in America followed the Wesleyan pattern of class meetings with lay leaders. Methodists in America, as in Great Britain itself, were tied to the Church of England. The Methodist preachers followed Wesley's instruction not to give the sacraments, and advised their members to partake of the sacraments at the Church of England. Yet, not all preachers agreed with this policy. They found few Anglican ministers interested in the spiritual and moral rigor that Methodism represented. To the consternation of both Wesley and Asbury, Robert Strawbridge, among others, offered the sacraments.

The first American Methodist Conference was held in Philadelphia in 1773. Thomas Rankin, who had just arrived as Wesley's "general assistant," presided. There were 1,160 members, with the highest concentration in Maryland.

During the Revolutionary War, Rankin and the other preachers that Wesley had sent to America returned to England—all except Francis Asbury. Wesley opposed the American Revolution, and, given the attachment of Methodism to the Church of England, colonists suspected that Methodists' loyalties rested with the Crown rather than with the cause of liberty. As a result, Asbury remained mostly in Delaware, traveling little during the war.

As soon as the war was over, Asbury returned to itinerant evangelism. Not always were there great results, as when he preached to "whiskey drinkers"[2] in western Virginia, to "unengaged"[3] hearers in Pennsylvania, or in "poor gospel-hardened Trenton,"[4] but Asbury's heart remained "enlarged and inflamed with love."[5] By 1783, two years after the Revolutionary War, the number of Methodists had risen to 82 preachers and 13,740 members.

By this time, Wesley realized that Methodism in America could not stay attached to the Church of England. For that reason, Wesley ordained Richard Whatcoat and Thomas Vasey for ministry in America and designated Thomas Coke—who was an ordained minister of the Church of England as well as one of Wesley's chief lieutenants—and Francis Asbury as co-superintendents. Wesley reduced the Thirty-Nine Articles of Religion of the Church of England to Twenty-Five Articles of Faith and revised the Sunday services of the Church of England for use in Methodist churches in America. However, Wesley's order of worship proved still too formal for the Americans.

At the 1784 "Christmas" Conference in Baltimore, considered the founding of Methodism in America, Coke, Whatcoat, and Vasey, with Philip Otterbein (a German Reformed minister also participating) ordained Asbury and others, first as deacons and then as elders. (The Methodists retained the Anglican system of ordaining a minister first as a deacon and then as an elder.) Asbury refused the appointment of superintendent, however, unless he were so elected by his fellow ministers. Asbury had won the support of the American preachers by his staying with them during the Revolutionary War. They proceeded to ratify Wesley's appointments of Asbury and Cook by electing them superintendents. Though Coke and Asbury were supposed to share the duties of the superintendency, Coke did not settle long in America and many responsibilities fell upon Asbury.

The ordination of Methodist ministers allowed them to administer the "ordinances" of the Lord's Supper and baptism. In North Carolina shortly after the Christmas Conference, Asbury himself both baptized infants and "plunged" four adult believers.[6]

LONGING FOR GOD

Asbury's *Journal,* which he maintained for four decades and intended for publication after his death, depicted a very human side, a man who suffered spiritual doubt and emotional depression, all the while pursuing holiness. Asbury's favorite text was 1 Timothy 1:15, "This is a faithful saying, and worthy of all acceptation, that Christ Jesus came into the world to save sinners; of whom I am chief" (KJV). Because Asbury often preached to sinners, his messages centered upon justification. Yet, Asbury did not neglect sanctification, and encouraged people into the experience.

The weariness of his body affected his soul, Asbury recognized, but sanctification came through suffering. Though he tried like Wesley to rise before 5:00 A.M. to study his Bible, illnesses, cold, and other impediments prevented him from always doing so. While hindered, he still longed to be more spiritual. One day after excessive labors, Asbury's bodily suffering prevented deep communion with God, he said, though he managed to read a few chapters in his Hebrew Bible. In South Carolina in 1794, though ill, Asbury ordained four elders and six deacons and preached to about 100. But they could not endure sound doctrine, Asbury felt, and he found himself in a "gloomy melancholy."[7] Nonetheless, Asbury saddled up and rode on, through swamps, cold, rain, and hunger, to his next assignment.

ADDRESSING SOCIAL CONDITIONS

Asbury's humble station and suffering allowed him to sympathize with others, even slaves. Early conferences banned Methodists from owning slaves. The egalitarian message of Methodists—that all could be saved—shook the hierarchy of authority that had captured, in particular, Southern society. From the beginning of his ministry in America, Asbury preached "deliverance to the captives" (Luke 4:18, KJV).

He persuaded conferences to establish Sunday Schools for poor children—both white and black. However, in the North as well as in the South, segregation marred Methodist brotherhood. A 1794 Conference in Virginia saw much discussion on slavery. The preachers decided not to own slaves whenever they were allowed to free them, and to pay them for labor where they were not allowed to free them. Finally, Methodism accommodated itself to slavery, allowing members to be slaveholders. Asbury grieved over Methodists who hired out their slaves to the highest bidder.

In 1799, Asbury ordained Richard Allen, a free African-American leader in Philadelphia, as a deacon. He ordained other "Africans," such as in Pennsylvania, in 1809, when he ordained Jacob Tapsco and James Champion. In the long run, though, Asbury gave up challenging slavery so as to freely evangelize both slaves and their masters. Richard Allen organized the separate African Methodist Episcopal Church and was ordained a bishop on April 11, 1816—11 days after Asbury's death.

SETTING AN EXAMPLE

Asbury and other Methodist bishops and preachers moved about constantly among the people. Asbury came to know Methodists—and Americans—as no one else. He set an example for every other Methodist preacher in accepting any and all hardships for the sake of evangelizing the people. Asbury lived frugally and admonished the same of others. He owned no property except his horse and belongings little enough to stuff in his saddle bags. He had a message of salvation to get across to the people, and the accommodations did not matter much. Asbury stayed with families—some rich, some extremely poor—or slept outdoors, in all kinds of weather conditions when necessary, in order to take the gospel to the people.

Like Asbury, in the initial years of their growth, Methodists lived differently from their neighbors. Methodists sensed themselves to be "a people set apart in opposition to the world."[8] They gave up drinking alcohol, for instance, dueling, dancing, theaters and circuses, jewelry, finery and frivolity, and observed the Lord's Day in order to maintain moral distinction between themselves and the surrounding culture.

Methodists found among themselves sufficient joy and peace. Methodists' speech, testimonies, and "love feasts"—in which members expressed verbally their affection for and shared bread with each other—deepened spiritual fellowship.

Even conferences lent themselves easily to camp meetings, and were occasions of great outpourings of the Spirit.

Asbury oversaw a vast and rapidly expanding system of circuits and preaching stations. The structure of Methodism allowed Asbury and later bishops freedom to quickly deploy preachers wherever and whenever needs arose, and enabled Methodism, more than any other denomination, to keep pace with the moving American population. When the number of souls and preaching points over which an itinerant had charge became too large, Asbury divided the circuit and appointed another itinerant.

Beginning in 1785, Asbury appointed "presiding elders" to oversee the work of several circuit riders. In order to maintain mobility, Asbury hoped that his preachers would remain, as he, single. As a missionary force under Asbury's command, Methodism functioned as effectively as a Roman Catholic order, taking hold of the North American continent through a cadre of young, dedicated, and enthusiastic evangelists. Methodism gave these young men far-reaching spiritual authority. They astounded new settlers on remote homesteads with their sudden presence. As late as 1809, of the 84 preachers in the Virginia Conference, only three were married.

Since the preachers only reached certain places once every month or six weeks, the spiritual care of the people was in the hands of laypersons, who visited the sick and grieving, maintained class meetings, taught Sunday School, and conducted worship services. The itinerant preachers often encountered laypersons having the experience of entire sanctification, a blessing that the young itinerants themselves may not have yet attained. In some cases, spiritual "mothers," widows with whom they stayed along their way, prayed for them and brought them into the experience of grace.

Preachers of other denominations had to adapt both their theology and preaching style to compete with the Methodist circuit riders, who spoke passionately and without sermon manuscripts. Though they did not originate revivals and camp meetings, Methodists put these new measures to great use.

The "settled" phase of American Methodism, when preachers preferred to raise families and live in towns rather than be about the task of raw evangelism, saddened Asbury. They were no longer able or willing to itinerate in the same ways in which they had done when they remained single. In the South, they no longer criticized slavery and patriarchal power structures. In a sense, they no longer meddled in society, allowing each man to dominate his household—its women as well as its slaves. Eventually, Methodism's settled pastors not only embraced the virtues of "honor," but tolerated its many vices.

Though a few ministers were well-educated for the time, most were recruited from among the common people. As Wesley had, the American Methodists published material and formed a course of study to educate these preachers while they were in ministry. Asbury set an example by reading various theological and historical books, as well as Wesley's sermons, while traveling.

AN ENDURING LEGACY

Wherever it planted itself in America, Methodism offered a common religious culture. The theology of Methodism, stressing individual responsibility, immediate salvation, equality before God, and the possibility of salvation for all, fit the mind-set of the American culture. Methodists prized values that enabled persons to succeed in an increasingly democratic society, those of innovation and ingenuity, initiative and optimism, mobility and organization. At the same time, Methodism challenged spiritual and all other forms of elitism and encouraged adherents to be actively engaged in determining their own destinies. That is, the message of Methodism as much as its organization enabled it to win America. Wesleyanism, in comparison to Calvinism, sped up the process and intensified the experience of conversion. Methodism boldly offered grace that not only was given freely for all, but that led sinners to repentance and believers toward holiness of life—not by a slow process, but immediate and radical transformation. One writer said, "It was loyalty to John Wesley's understanding of the 'circumcision of the heart' that made a Methodist a Methodist."[9]

As Asbury made his way from conference to conference, he shared news of revival, which inspired other revivals. In later years, word of Asbury's coming to a locality was sufficient in itself to attract listeners. About 1,500 persons, one-fourth of the population, turned out to hear him in Fayetteville, North Carolina, for instance. Three thousand persons attended a camp meeting at Brownsville, Pennsylvania, pitching tents and wagons.[10] At such meetings, Methodists shouted and experienced visions. It was not always easy, however, to promote revival. At a camp meeting in New York, Asbury had to deal with drunk young men who were harassing the meetings.

Early preachers and evangelists remained accessible to the people. Any Methodist home, no matter how humble, might enjoy the company of Bishop Asbury as well as other itinerants. This became less common as the church grew. At the same time, domestic family life and midweek prayer services took the place of the class meetings.

In a culture increasingly dominated in many places by Methodists, there were fewer distinctions between the world and the church. These situations in part provoked the holiness movement. In some of his last speeches and letters, Asbury warned Methodists of accommodating to the winds and whims of culture. In his last *Journal* entry, December 7, 1815, Asbury wrote: "My consolations are great. I live in God from moment to moment."[11] Three months later, on March 31, 1816, in Richmond, Virginia, he died.

Within 50 years, from 1770 to 1820, Methodists increased from fewer than 1,000 members to 250,000. Soon after Asbury's death, within one decade, Methodism doubled this, reaching 500,000 members by 1830. By 1850, Methodists made up 34 percent of Protestants in America, 50 percent more than the Baptists, their nearest rival, and 10 times the number of Congregationalists. More than to anyone else, the triumph of Methodism in American culture was due to Francis Asbury, a man who "made an offer of myself."

Notes:

1. Francis Asbury, *The Journal and Letters of Francis Asbury*, vol. 1 (Nashville: Abingdon, 1958), 3.

2. Asbury. *Journal*, vol. 1, 406.

3. Asbury. *Journal*, vol. 1, 431.

4. Asbury. *Journal*, vol. 1, 431.

5. Asbury. *Journal*, vol. 1, 254.

6. Asbury. *Journal*, vol. 1, 480-81.

7. Asbury. *Journal*, vol. 2, 6.

8. John Wigger, *Taking Heaven by Storm* (London: Oxford University Press, 1998), 192.

9. Dee Andrews, *The Methodists and Revolutionary America*, (Princeton, N.J.: Princeton University Press, 2000), 239.

10. Asbury. *Journal*, vol. 2, 646.

11. Asbury. *Journal*, vol. 2, 797.

Scripture Cited: Luke 4:18; 1 Timothy 1:15

PHOEBE PALMER: HOLINESS MATRIARCH

(19TH CENTURY)
BY DIANE LECLERC

Phoebe Worrall was born December 18, 1807. Her father, Henry Worrall became a Methodist in Yorkshire, England, as a teenager, without the rest of his family. He boasted of receiving his class ticket from John Wesley himself, which was a card that recognized one's loyalty to the Methodist cause. As a young man, Worrall immigrated to America, and continued his Methodist devotion. He met another young Methodist, Dorothea Wade, and married her. They had 16 children, 8 of which survived to adulthood. Phoebe was the 4th of the 8.

Their home is described as a place of intense religious devotion. For the Worralls, family worship came at least two times a day. Besides the home, Phoebe's spiritual development was directly influenced by the family's involvement in their Methodist church. A significant figure for the rest of her life was Nathan Bangs, who taught Phoebe her catechism in 1817. By all accounts, her spirituality developed at a very early age, and showed unusual maturity in her understanding of theology and in holiness of life. Later, her writings would evidence deep insights into Scripture and holiness theology, despite only an eighth-grade education.

In 1826, Phoebe met Walter Clarke Palmer, who wondered whether he should prepare for the ministry. He then became convinced that being a pious physician would be a very Christlike occupation. So, he completed his medical studies and embarked on three "projects": establishing a medical practice, leading the Sunday School at the Allen Street Methodist Episcopal Church, and winning the hand of Phoebe Worrall. Palmer saw medical care as a ministry. Besides offering testimony of his Christian commitment to his patients, he also ministered by giving free care to the poor and by financially supporting many different charitable causes.

Walter and Phoebe married on September 28, 1827. While it has been said that the Palmers were both well-suited in interest and personality, and that they maintained a quite blissful marriage, their lives were not without difficulty, even great tragedy.

On their first wedding anniversary, Phoebe gave birth to a son, Alexander. Thus began a spiritual struggle that deeply shaped her developing theology. By her own admission, she put off having him baptized, because she could not admit publicly that she was giving him to God without reservation. This brought intense guilt when the baby died 11 months later. She felt that he had been *taken* away forcefully, not *given* up willingly. She did not question God, but acknowledged her own "idolatry." A few months later, the Palmers had a second son, Samuel. One can speculate that this time she saw herself as Hannah, willingly giving up *her* Samuel to God. Unfortunately, he lived only seven weeks. Her understanding of this experience as another deep failure of "idolatry" compelled her to vow never to make this mistake again.

Her theology is way off here. She thought that God took the children as punishment for her sin, which we do not believe. And yet, this experience and those to come did, in fact, shape a crucial element of her theology of surrender and consecration in the work of sanctification.

Her spiritual struggles continued, despite a new resolve to press on. She was raised Methodist and had inherited an

Americanized version of Wesley's call to Christian holiness. And yet, Palmer found such a quest very hard and confusing, for she believed herself to have always been and, therefore, never quite a Christian. She had not had a powerful conversion experience and had no definite assurance of her standing with God, which was required to "go on to perfection." She would not attain witness of the Spirit (assurance) until after the next unthinkable tragedy.

Her first daughter, Sarah, was born in 1833. A second daughter was born in 1835. Phoebe's travail returned as both she and this child, Eliza, were very sick, to the point of near-death. This brush with death gave her a new perspective on life. She no longer had fears about her eternal destiny, but she hoped that she would not die so she could have more time to live for God.

Unfortunately, unimaginable suffering struck again. After Phoebe and Eliza recovered, a maid was careless with an oil lamp and set Eliza's crib on fire. Phoebe held her daughter, still conscious, until she died a few hours later. She felt God very near to her, in a very unusual way, as she wept and mourned. Whatever she experienced, the result was new determination to do Christ's work with all the time she would have spent on the child. She also seems to have reached the assurance that she had so craved. This paved the way for seeking entire sanctification more deeply.

THE TURNING POINT

Palmer finally reached that "day of days." She records the following in her diary on July 26, 1837:

> On the morning of this day . . . my thought rested more especially upon the beloved one whom God had given to be the partner of my life. How truly a gift from God, and how essentially connected with my spiritual, as also my temporal, happiness is this one dear object! I exclaimed. Scarcely had these suggestions passed, when

with keenness these inquiries were suggested: "Have you not professedly given up all for Christ? If he who now so truly absorbs affections were required, would you not shrink from the demand?" I need not say that this one dear object, though often in name surrendered, was not in reality given up. My precious little ones, whom God had taken to himself, were then brought to my recollection, as if to admonish me relative to making the sacrifice. I thought how fondly *I had idolized them.* He who had said, "I the Lord your God am a jealous God," saw the *idolatry* of my heart, and took them to himself. The remembrance of how decidedly I had, by these repeated bereavements, been assured that He whose right it is to reign, would be the sole sovereign of my heart, assisted me in the resolve, that neither should this, the yet dearer object, be withheld . . . In full view of the nature of the sacrifice, I said "take life or friends away." I could just as readily have said, "take life," as I could have said "take friends"; for that which was just as dear, if not dearer, than life, had been required. And when I said, "Take him who is the supreme object of my earthly affection," I, from that moment felt that I was fully set apart for God.[1]

Palmer attributed sanctification's delay to a lack of realization of the "depth" and gravity of truly surrendering her "idols." In a letter to a friend, she said:

> With Abraham I said, "I have lifted my hand to the Lord." In a word, I had again and again made the sacrifice before, and said, "My husband and child I surrender to thee." I had not been insincere, but I now saw that I had not in fact done that which, in word, had often been named. Far indeed, had I been from realizing the depth of obligation which, in word, I had taken upon myself.[2]

After realizing precisely what was required and after reaching the moment of complete surrender, Palmer finally believed herself entirely sanctified and free from the bondage of sin. This day, founded upon her interpretation of incredible tragedy, was, without a doubt, a turning point in Phoebe Palmer's life and vocation, and for the American Holiness Movement.

SHARING THE BLESSING

Palmer began from this point to formulate her own experience into a theology to be shared with others. It was after this experience that Palmer's life began to change and expand in significant, even incredible, ways. The Palmers had moved into a house on the lower east side of New York City and begun living with Phoebe's sister Sarah and her husband, Thomas Lankford. After Sarah's sanctification experience, she combined two women's meetings into one that met on Tuesday mornings in their home. It was a period of time when their local Methodist church was experiencing great revival. At the first meeting, Sarah was astonished to see many, even notable, Methodist women find radical victory in prayer. Those Tuesday meetings have sometimes been credited for the holiness revival that sprang forth and expanded for decades to come. It is certainly true that when Phoebe assumed leadership and the meetings began to include men, some of the most prominent Methodist leaders of the 19th century were influenced by what happened in that parlor, many attending themselves. The meetings also influenced many major religious leaders who were not Methodists.

Palmer's acclaim quickly expanded. For the next 30-plus years, her ministry was widespread—theologically rigorous, dynamically revivalistic, and socially relevant. Besides traveling extensively throughout the United States—preaching at revivals and, later, camp meetings—she also spent several years abroad in the same vocation. It could be said that she brought the meaning of sanctification back to the land of Wesley. Her name would have been synonymous with the higher-life movement that spread throughout the British Isles. She is thought to be a revivalist of the caliber and popularity of Charles Finney himself. Twenty-five thousand were converted, and thousands upon thousands sanctified, under her evangelistic ministry. She also wrote dozens of books and tracts, as well as editing the most influential holiness magazine of the century. She started the famous Five Points inner-city mission and made charity work commonplace. She was influential in Methodist higher education, and never considered herself anything but staunchly faithful to the Methodist tradition, and to Wesley himself.

THE SHORTER WAY

Palmer is most well-known for what is called the "altar covenant" which was a way of describing her own experience. This concept is most clearly seen in her famous book, *The Way of Holiness.* Palmer's motivation for this work was to help others who also had possibly struggled with finding an assurance about their sanctification. It clearly served this purpose for her and for many who embraced her teachings. This altar covenant reduced what could be a complicated and perplexing search for holiness into what she termed a "shorter way."

Palmer took Adam Clarke's commentary note on Exodus 29:37 and applied it to the experience of sanctification. Clarke explains that in Hebrew ritual, whatever was laid upon the altar became God's possession; it was from then on to be used for sacred purposes. Clarke describes Christ as the altar. According to Palmer's scheme, a person who seeks entire sanctification must first and foremost consecrate, or surrender, everything completely to God by "placing" all (all of one's being and all of one's "idols") on God's "altar." After this consecration is complete, the seeker must then have faith that the "altar sanctifies the gift."

This might sound as if we do all the work. Yet, Palmer

affirms that one's ability to turn from idols, consecrate everything, and "believe the promise" is not accomplished through human ability, but rather through one's reception of God's prevenient grace. She writes often of the absolute necessity of grace. Her assertion of faith is filled with language of God's prior, prevenient action, specifically through His Spirit. Some have called Palmer's ideas here overly simplistic and too much like a forced formula. This might be true. However, for thousands and thousands of people during her lifetime and later, her ideas provided a means for experiencing and understanding sanctification.

POWER TO CHANGE

"Holiness is power" is an often repeated phrase in Palmer's writings. The disciples in Acts were empowered by the Spirit to accomplish what was impossible without divine assistance. Present-day people who experienced entire sanctification were empowered also to accomplish what was beyond their own human limitations. According to Palmer, through empowerment and "unhindered" freedom, a person was enabled to progress in his or her spiritual journey as never before and to accomplish what was beyond human expectation or conventional custom. This was particularly significant for women's Christian experience. Women began to see their own potential for ministry and usefulness in church and society, and started to challenge structures that would limit them.

Palmer affirmed that Christians were not only justified before God, but were also regenerate, reborn, made new, capable of being restored to the state in which God created human beings. And so, the argument that "this is the way we've always done it," holds no power for someone for whom all things have been made new. Limitations are determined only by one's own disobedience. As a result of this theological idea, women began to strive toward the realization of the "new life" they claimed. These women believed they had equal access to the "Pentecostal power" available through the Holy Spirit; they were equally capable to be "Pentecostal witnesses" to what God can do in a life that is entirely devoted. To be empowered through sanctifying grace compelled women to enter the sphere of society and effect change. It often meant ministering to the physical needs of others, especially to those of a lower social position, as evidenced by Palmer's strong emphasis on mission work. But it also meant that sanctifying power meant empowerment to speak.

Sacrifice could mean a giving up, but also a willingness to do it. For Palmer, self-sacrifice did not mean playing the typical, martyr-like role of the subservient wife and mother. This, in fact, would have been the *easiest* or "widest" road, in her mind. Rather, sacrifice meant being *courageous* in the secular sphere: it was a personal sacrifice for a woman to be considered "undignified" by society for overstepping her feminine boundaries. Still, such an undignified position, according to Palmer, was *required* by God. And so holiness women were allowing themselves to view this self-development as part of their Christian duty, rather than something egotistical or evil. It is not coincidental, then, that almost all of the new holiness denominations that were forming in the last part of the 19th century ordained women right from the beginning.

AN ENDURING MESSAGE

Phoebe Palmer would have been a household name in America during her lifetime. She can certainly be considered the matriarch of the Holiness Movement. Particularly her writing and preaching ministry changed the religious landscape of America. More importantly, thousands upon thousands of lives were changed because of the message of holiness. Palmer made that message a bit easier to understand, and we still proclaim it over a hundred years later. There may be theological squabbles about the fine points of her theology, but overall, Palmer affirmed how our lives are deeply changed when we are entirely devoted to God. That message will never get old.

Notes:

1. Thomas C. Oden, ed., *Phoebe Palmer: Selected Writings* (New York: Paulist Press, 1988), 36 (italics added).

2. Oden, 114-15.

11

PHINEAS BRESEE: IN ALL THINGS CHARITY

(EARLY 20TH CENTURY)
BY FLOYD CUNNINGHAM

At age 56, after 37 years of ministry in the Methodist Episcopal Church, Phineas Bresee found himself without a church.

In September 1895, as he made his way by train back home to Los Angeles after preaching in holiness camp meetings in the eastern United States, he pondered what God would have him do. Meeting him at the train station when he arrived was a faithful band of supporters, including some who had prayed for him ever since he and his family had arrived in California 12 years before.

Bresee and his followers soon decided to start an independent mission to preach holiness to the poor, whom they thought were being neglected by other churches. On October 6, 1895, the mission began. Bresee's friend, Joseph P. Widney, chose the proper name of the mission, "Church of the Nazarene." "Nazarene," used in derision, signified the toiling, lowly mission of Jesus, and the way in which Bresee and his followers linked their vision to the looked-down-upon Carpenter from despised Nazareth.

Bresee had come to Los Angeles after pastoring in Iowa for 26 years, but his life began in Franklin, New York, on December 31, 1838. Even before his conversion in a Methodist revival in February 1856, Bresee knew he was to be a minister. Soon after his conversion, the Methodist conference licensed Bresee as an "exhorter," and he began preaching.

BRESEE THE IOWA METHODIST PASTOR

Methodism was strong in Iowa and included some of the leading citizens of the state. Bresee became a well-known and respected figure in the Iowa Methodist Conference.

To begin, Bresee assisted an older preacher, and then was appointed to a circuit. Like other Methodist preachers, Bresee changed circuits every year or so. In 1859, Bresee was ordained a deacon. The following year, Bresee returned to New York to marry Maria Hibbard. While serving the Grinnell Circuit, Bresee was ordained an elder. On the Galesburg Circuit, Bresee took in 140 members. He then became pastor of the First Methodist Church in Des Moines, the state capitol. When Bresee was only 25, the bishop appointed him presiding elder (the equivalent of a district superintendent) over a portion of Western Iowa. Then Bresee returned to pastoring. While serving in Chariton, Bresee experienced a spiritual breakthrough which, though undefined at that time, he later referred to as his "baptism with the Holy Ghost." With increased effectiveness in his ministry, revivals and strong church growth followed wherever he ministered. Always, Bresee considered evangelism to be the chief task of the pastor. At the same time, Bresee encouraged Methodist education and helped to establish Simpson College. Bresee again pastored in Des Moines, and then in Council Bluffs, Red Oak, Clarinda, Creston, and, once more, in Council Bluffs. In several of these places, Bresee erected substantial church buildings. Some thought him on his way to becoming a bishop.

However, during his later years in Iowa, Bresee invested in a Mexican silver mine and promoted it among Methodist pastors and laypersons. Either other investors duped him (there is some indication that the mine might never have existed), or else the mine was destroyed by a flood. In any event, Bresee lost his money, his reputation among Iowa Methodists, and confidence in his spiritual leadership. He decided to move to California, and vowed to repay those who had invested money in the mine.

BRESEE THE CALIFORNIA METHODIST PASTOR

California offered new beginnings and new hope for many. Los Angeles itself was a booming city. By 1883, "Anglos" out-numbered the once-dominant Mexican population. From a population of only 11,000 in 1880, Los Angeles grew to over 50,000 by 1890 (and reached 450,000 by the time of Bresee's death 25 years later).

Friends from Iowa who preceded Bresee prepared the way for him to be appointed pastor of the First Methodist Church in Los Angeles soon after his arrival. A strong lay faction was committed to holiness. In 1884, after revivals with leaders of the National Camp Meeting Association for the Promotion of Holiness, Bresee experienced a transforming event (that he rarely talked about) in which he "swallowed" a burning ball of light. This led to renewed power in his ministry.

Among those who were equally swayed by the message of holiness was J. P. Widney, a medical doctor, real estate investor, prohibition activist, and one of the most prominent leaders of Southern California society. Widney had been instrumental in founding the University of Southern California in 1880, and Bresee became one of USC's trustees.

Bresee remained as pastor of L. A. First Methodist until 1886, when he was transferred to the Methodist church in Pasadena. While pastoring there over the next four years, he raised the membership of the church from 130 to 1,000. Part of the holiness message, to Bresee and others, involved the continued reformation of society. To this effect, Bresee joined the Prohibition Party and campaigned to make Pasadena "dry."

In the meantime, Bresee repaid those who had invested in the silver mine. No longer motivated by anything material, if he left his house in the morning with money in his pocket, there would be none left when he returned at the end of the day, because he would have given it all to needy persons.

Bresee was assigned to Asbury Church in Los Angeles in 1890, and, the following year, the bishop appointed Bresee presiding elder, with the understanding that Bresee would promote holiness revivals. Over the next year, Bresee again brought in National Camp Meeting Association evangelists, and Southern California Methodism burned with revival.

Holiness teachings became controversial within the Methodist Church. Though the bishop warmly supported the movement, his successor saw the issue as divisive. He appointed Bresee to the Simpson Church, where the bishop knew Bresee would have difficulties. The church had gotten itself into debt during an overly ambitious building program. Bresee could not bring revival to the congregation. He was not much more successful the following year among the people of the Boyle Heights church. He no longer felt welcome or comfortable in the denomination that he had served for so many years.

Bresee increasingly felt himself called to Los Angeles's poor, many of them migrants from farms. Bresee desired that his conference, in 1894, allow him to work with others to begin the Peniel Mission. This was to be an undenominational work, but warm to holiness. The conference was suspicious that the mission would draw Methodists away from their own churches. So rather than an appointment, the conference gave Bresee what amounted to retired status. Bresee then embarked on a wide-ranging evangelistic tour. While away, he received word that his services were no longer needed at the Peniel Mission. When Bresee arrived in Los Angeles in September 1895, he was a man without a church.

BRESEE AS FOUNDER OF THE CHURCH OF THE NAZARENE

Los Angeles First Church of the Nazarene, pastored by Bresee until 1911, became one of the cornerstones of the denomination eventually bearing its name. The church started as a mission—not unlike countless other urban store-front holiness missions.

At an early church meeting, members elected Bresee and Widney general superintendents for life. However, Widney left the fledgling denomination after only three years. Bresee renounced his election "for life" and allowed himself to be put forward for reelection at each succeeding general assembly.

The rented hall gave way in 1896 to a plain board structure, known as the "glory barn," which seated 400. Bresee desired that all say "welcome" to the poor. Well aware of other independent holiness congregations and associations throughout the country, Bresee promoted "organized holiness" or "come-out-ism" through his paper, which, like other holiness periodicals of the time, helped to bind the movement together. At the same time, the church established missions among Chinese and Mexicans.

After having been instrumental in promoting several schools while a Methodist minister, Bresee was hesitant to begin a Nazarene college. Only when several women in his congregation organized a school for Christian workers did Bresee take interest. The school opened in September 1902, and moved to Pasadena four years later. (The university that Pasadena College grew into is now located in Point Loma.) Bresee saw the school as consistent with the mission of the church. He desired to give poor persons the opportunity for education. Bresee wanted the school to be filled with such holy fire that students would experience entire sanctification and take a burning passion for the lost back to local congregations. He also affirmed that the school was not to be "sectarian," and in the first several years the student body represented 15 denominations. Firmly committed to holiness, Bresee saw the importance of the liberal arts. In 1915, the year of Bresee's death, the school enrolled 443 students, representing 23 states and 6 foreign countries.

While those who attended Bresee's Church of the Nazarene were committed to ministry among poor people, not all were themselves poor. Most were middle class. God did not intend for His people to be poverty-stricken, Bresee said in one of his sermons from Matthew, but His grace made them industrious, frugal, honest, and wise people of prayer.

The government of the church was democratic. Church discipline depended upon the conviction of the Holy Spirit, and the church's few written rules reflected the ethos of early American Methodism. They included honoring the Lord's Day by refraining from unnecessary labor or business; avoiding using intoxicating liquors or "trafficking" in the same; avoiding dishonesty—taking advantage of others in buying or selling; and refraining from prideful dress and living. There were informal admonishments regarding membership in secret societies and the use of tobacco.

Lucy P. Knott organized about 400 young women into "Company E," while the young men's group was known as the "Brotherhood of St. Stephen." The young people visited hospitals. Sunday School scholars gathered for picnics. Knott started a church on Mateo Street, and Bresee quickly saw the wisdom of ordaining this woman and other women for ministry. Over the next few years, he not only defended the right of women to be ordained, but postponed union with other holiness organizations that saw differently on this issue.

Bresee's personality and leadership left a deep imprint. Bresee committed to memory the Bible books of Isaiah, John, and Hebrews, and scripture permeated his sermons.

Bresee gathered notes for his Sunday sermons throughout the week, from literature, history, newspapers, and his members' life situations. He wove these thoughts together and wrote out his sermons in a nearly complete manuscript. Then he would soak in its message, and commit the outline to memory. Leaving the manuscript in his study, Bresee seemed to preach extemporaneously. Bresee pointed out that the best sermon preparation was the spiritual readiness of the preacher.

Bresee understood himself to be preaching no novel doctrines, only the teachings of Methodism's great founder, John Wesley. The *doctrine* of holiness was important to Bresee, since entire sanctification was central to the reason and being of the Church of the Nazarene, and was what, he feared, the Methodists were losing. But the *experience* of holiness was even more crucial.

Bresee did not assume that all members were in the experience of entire sanctification. He sought to lead them into the grace by resuscitating Wesley's class meetings, Methodism's love feasts, and Phoebe Palmer's Tuesday holiness meetings, and by incorporating some elements of the camp meeting. A band that included trumpets and trombones accompanied lively gospel singing. Bresee, not known for his singing, clapped his hands along with the music. Bresee could not countenance superficiality, however, and could tell the difference between emotion and true spirituality. Like camp meetings, every Nazarene worship service could lead to an "altar call," through which, in prayer around the kneeling rail, persons might be born again, entirely sanctified, or brought closer to Christ.

Bresee tied himself firmly to his Los Angeles congregation, but encouraged his coworkers to build bridges to other groups for the sake of "organized holiness." In 1907, his associate, C. W. Ruth, forged links between the Church of the Nazarene and the Association of Pentecostal Churches of America, which was centered around Brooklyn and Boston.

Bresee himself went east to meet these holiness people with whom he had so much in common, and the union was consummated in Chicago in October 1907. Bresee also personally visited Peniel, Texas, site of Texas Holiness University, and persuaded the local congregation to unite with the Church of the Nazarene. However, the birth of the denomination came in October 1908 at Pilot Point, Texas, with the union of the Church of the Nazarene and the Holiness Church of Christ, which was strongest in Tennessee, Arkansas, and Texas.

The church's beliefs were the common, orthodox doctrines of the Church on the Trinity, sin, the atonement, justification, and sanctification. Bresee admonished people not to concentrate upon or to divide over "non-essentials." The Church of the Nazarene drew in members from other denominations—Presbyterians and Quakers, as well as Baptists and Methodists—who had a variety of opinions about some "non-essential" issues, but who were united in their experience of entire sanctification. For instance, Bresee, like Methodists, baptized infants. Others baptized only believers. The Nazarene *Manual* provided for baptizing both infants and adults. The mode of baptism, whether by sprinkling, pouring, or immersing, was optional. Though Nazarenes believed in the second coming of Christ, they did not specify the timing of it, and Nazarenes could be postmillennialists (like Bresee) or premillennialists or amillennialists. Though Nazarenes believed in divine healing, they did not emphasize this or make it the center of their evangelistic meetings, fearing that this would supplant the centrality of heart purity. Many of the issues that divided other Christians were not "essential" to Nazarenes. Bresee borrowed from Rupertus Meldenius, an obscure 17th-century German theologian, the phrase that characterized what he desired for the Church of the Nazarene as it sought to embody the spirit of the Holiness Movement: "In essentials unity, in non-essentials liberty, in all things charity (love)."

12

THE EMERGENCE OF EVANGELICALS

(MID-20TH CENTURY)
BY C. S. COWLES

A dairy farmer offered a secluded corner of his pasture to his Christian businessmen's Bible study group for a day of prayer. Out of that prayer meeting came the Greater Charlotte Evangelistic Crusade. On the last verse of "Almost Persuaded," sung after all the verses of "Just As I Am," that dairyman's "lean and lanky" 16-year-old son walked down the long aisle and made his decision for Christ. Little did he realize that his son would preach the gospel to more people in more places over a longer period of time than any other 100 evangelists in history. Largely because of Billy Graham's astonishing ministry, evangelicals have emerged from the shadows of a backwater Christian subculture into the bright lights of ecclesial, national, and world prominence. And the impact has been incalculable.

FUNDAMENTALISM'S MIXED LEGACY

Mid-20th-century evangelicalism was bracketed between the infamous Scopes "Monkey Trial" in 1925 and the election of Jimmy Carter as the first evangelical president of the United States in 1975. The Scopes trial, which convicted a high school biology teacher for teaching Darwinian evolution, thrust onto center-stage the furious liberal-conservative battle that had been waged in Protestant churches for nearly a century. In order to sharpen their identity as defenders of historic Christian orthodoxy, evangelicals published a collection of essays written by 64 British and American scholars, called *The Fundamentals: A Testimony to Truth* (1910-1915). From this 12-volume set, the editors distilled five core doctrinal beliefs that have defined evangelicals ever since. They are the inerrancy of the Scriptures, the Virgin Birth and deity of Christ, the substitutionary atonement, the miracles and bodily resurrection of Jesus, and the premillennial second coming of Christ. H. L. Mencken, acerbic journalist of the early 20th century, derisively dubbed these evangelicals "Fundamentalists." The label stuck.

Having either withdrawn from or been frozen out of mainline denominations, embattled fundamentalists established their own churches, Bible colleges, seminaries, missionary organizations, publishing companies, and numerous parachurch organizations. In reaction to the rising tide of liberalism within the church and secular humanism without, they morphed into an increasingly sectarian and separatist movement. They were fiercely anti-Catholic; refused to associate with "Modernists"; defended racial segregation; denied ordination to women; renounced the use of alcohol and tobacco; forbade gambling, card-playing, dancing, and movies; practiced strict observance of the Sabbath; and railed against "looseness" in dress and behavior. This was the movement into which Billy Graham was born, raised, and nurtured.

The genius of evangelicals, however, was not so much their devotion to doctrinal "fundamentals" as their spiritual dynamism centered in a transformational "born again" experience with Christ. Few have personified its vitality more clearly than its most visible representative. Billy started witnessing to his fellow classmates the day after making his decision for Christ, began having daily devotions, and became involved in a Tuesday night teen Bible study group. Within weeks, he was asked to give his testimony at a youth group, in a prison, and to young girls in a home for unwed mothers.

So eager was he to share Christ that he witnessed to strangers, preached on street corners, and held services at a trailer park, where he was soon drawing crowds of 200 and 300. He exemplified all that was best in the evangelicalism of his youth.

Upon graduation from high school, he enrolled at Bob Jones College. There, he encountered fundamentalism's darker side: its legalism, narrowness, and fortress mentality. Frustrated by the college's rigidity and stifling intellectual climate, he voiced his complaints. Bob Jones Sr., founder and president of the college, called him into his office. "You are a failure," he boomed, "and will be nothing but a failure!" Billy was so demoralized by the dressing down that he dropped out after the first semester.

We may never have heard of Billy Graham had it not been for John Minder, dean and professor of Bible at Florida Bible College, to which he transferred. Professor Minder not only became his chief encourager, but opened the door for him to preach in nearby churches. It was not long until he was holding revivals. After one such meeting in 1939, he was ordained a Southern Baptist minister, virtually by acclamation. He finished his education at Wheaton College, where a more open and winsome expression of evangelicalism flourished.

EMERGENCE OF THE NEW EVANGELICALS

While scores of pastors, scholars, and leaders contributed to shaping what evangelicals have become today, two others in addition to Billy Graham stand out. They launched movements and established institutions that continue to exert enormous influence today.

Charles E. Fuller

Seeing the vast potential that radio offered in extending the reach of his preaching ministry, Charles E. Fuller resigned his pastorate in 1937, and devoted himself to full-time radio preaching. His first broadcast was carried on 13 stations. By the close of World War II, the Old Fashioned Revival Hour was being aired on 650 stations, making him the most influential preacher in America. I grew up listening to him on Sunday afternoons.

Charles E. Fuller's legacy lives on in the way evangelicals have utilized all forms of media to spread the gospel, and most importantly in Fuller Theological Seminary, founded in 1947. His vision was that the seminary would break out of the intellectually arid and socially isolationist culture of fundamentalism's past, and would become the flagship of evangelical scholarship. With its nearly 4,500 students from 67 countries representing 108 denominations, it has not only become our country's largest seminary, but has fulfilled his dream beyond what he could ever have imagined. Its faculty members have earned the respect of Christian scholars everywhere, and its graduates include such leading evangelical luminaries as Bill Bright of Campus Crusade, John Wimber of the Vineyard Church movement, and numerous megachurch pastors, such as Rick Warren, author of the best-selling *The Purpose-Driven Life*.

Henrietta Mears

For 35 years, Henrietta Mears (1928-1963) reigned as the dean of evangelical women, and wielded unprecedented influence as director of Christian education at Hollywood Presbyterian Church. She has been credited with doing more to dignify the work of Sunday Schools than any other person in history. She became one of the most popular and widely traveled Bible teachers of her generation. She authored numerous books and Bible study series.

On the eve of his historic Los Angeles Crusade in 1949, Billy Graham fought the battle of his life. After seeking and receiving wise counsel from Henrietta, he had a sanctifying encounter with God in which some troubling intellectual and spiritual issues were settled. He testifies that she had more influence on him than any other person, apart from his mother and wife.

Billy Graham

If a date can be fixed when evangelicalism broke free of its fundamentalist-separatist-segregationist bondage, it would be May 15, 1957, the opening day of Billy Graham's Greater New York Crusade. Scheduled for two weeks, it continued for two-and-a-half months. Attendance exceeded 2,000,000, breaking all previous records for any religious gathering. More than 61,000 people made decisions for Christ. Nothing like that had ever happened before.

The New York crusade proved to be a watershed event for three reasons. First, it marked *a clean break with extreme fundamentalism.* By accepting the call of the Protestant Council of New York, which was the local arm of the liberal National Council of Churches, Graham reached out across the great divide that had for so long separated evangelicals from the greater body of churches, including Catholic, and opened the door for an "ecumenism of spirit" that has been the hallmark of his ministry. In doing so, he earned the everlasting ire of doctrinaire fundamentalists, who, much to his sorrow, have been his most vitriolic critics ever since.

Second, the New York crusade marked *a decisive break with racial segregation.* Billy Graham not only invited Martin Luther King Jr. to offer an opening prayer, but commended him for his leadership in "a great social revolution." Noticing that the make-up of his audience was mostly white, Graham made preaching forays into Harlem. From then on, his crusade more nearly reflected the diverse racial composition of the city. Several years later, when local Atlanta crusade committee members divided the stadium into sections for blacks and whites, Billy Graham and his team members went through the stadium and tore down all the signs.

Third, the New York crusade *received unprecedented media exposure.* Coinciding with the advent of mass-marketed

television, millions who had only read about Billy Graham
in newspapers now saw him on TV. Not only did he capture
their attention and gain their respect, but he gave to evangelicalism a dynamic presence, a positive face, and a powerful
voice. The role he has played in the astonishing emergence
of evangelicals from the shadows to center-stage is beyond
all calculation.

AN UNEASY PARTNERSHIP

Are Wesleyans evangelicals? Yes and no. If "evangelical" is
understood in its New Testament sense as describing those
who proclaim the "good news" that "God was in Christ, reconciling the world unto himself" (2 Corinthians 5:19, KJV),
then Wesleyans are evangelical in the best sense of the word.
Wesleyans share with evangelicals everywhere the centrality of
the Scriptures, fidelity to historic Christian orthodoxy, the necessity of the new birth, the importance of Christian disciple-
ship, and the imperative to spread the gospel. Wesleyan denominations have wholeheartedly supported Billy Graham's
crusades and other similar evangelistic efforts, and most are
members of the National Association of Evangelicals.

On the other hand, Wesleyan denominations have been
wary of describing themselves as "evangelicals." The Church
of the Nazarene, for instance, has never defined itself as
"evangelical." The word does not even appear in its official
Manual, except as part of the name of a small holiness denomination that merged with it decades ago.

Why this reluctance? "From its beginnings, [the Church
of the Nazarene] has confessed itself to be a branch of the
'one, holy, universal, and apostolic' church and has sought to
be faithful to it. . . . It embraces the people of God through
the ages, those redeemed through Jesus Christ in whatever
expression of the one church they may be found."[1] This reflects a Wesleyan catholicity of spirit that most of today's
evangelicals find uncomfortable. The influential Evangelical

Theological Society, for instance, delineates its membership requirements so narrowly as to exclude most scholars from other Christian communions, including Wesleyans.

More pointedly, Wesleyans differ from contemporary mainstream evangelicals in three important areas. First, many evangelicals, reflecting their Calvinistic heritage and theological orientation, propagate a concept of God that Wesleyans find troubling—if not monstrous. No sooner had the twin towers of America's cathedral of capitalism crashed to the ground on September 11, 2001, than two highly visible evangelicals, Jerry Falwell and Pat Robertson, attributed the hijackings to God's judgment upon America on a *700 Club* telecast. Though both reversed themselves in the wake of the firestorm that followed, they were reflexively expressing their belief in the absolute sovereignty of God, the central tenant of John Calvin's theology. "God," Calvin wrote, "so regulates *all things* that *nothing takes place* without his deliberation."[2] That, of course, would include inciting hijackers to crash airliners into the World Trade Center towers and the Pentagon, killing over 3,000 people.

To attribute such atrocities to God, Wesleyans believe, is an outrage against His character. It makes Him, as Wesley protested in reacting to Calvin's doctrine of double predestination, "more false, more cruel, and more unjust than the devil. . . . God hath taken [Satan's] work out of [his] hands . . . God is the destroyer of souls."[3] Mennonite theologian Walter Wink writes, "Against such an image of God, the revolt of atheism is an act of pure religion."[4]

God's essence—the artesian well from which flow all of His attributes and actions—is *agape* love (see 1 John 4:8, 16). God is absolutely sovereign; yet for love's sake, He has limited His sovereignty at the point of human freedom. "God so *loved* the world," John tells us in the golden text of Christian theology and devotion, "that *he gave* his one and only Son, that *whoever* believes on him shall not perish but have everlasting life. For God did not send his Son into the world to

condemn the world, but to save the world through him"
(John 3:16-17, emphasis added). The God revealed fully and
finally in Jesus is one who would rather die than destroy human lives—and did (see Luke 9:51-56).

Second, the infallible Word in which Wesleyans place
their faith is *not a book, but Jesus, the Living Word,* to whom
the Bible gives faithful and true witness. "You search the
Scriptures," said Jesus to the scribes and Pharisees who were
biblical literalists to the core, "because you think that in them
you have eternal life; [yet] it is they that testify on my behalf"
(John 5:39, NRSV). Wesleyans are reluctant to ascribe "inerrancy" (a rationalistic, nonbiblical word) to the Bible in that
the Scriptures not only contain the testimony of "apostles and
prophets" but also the words of the serpent, Satan, demons,
pagans, idolaters, false prophets, fools, murderers, adulterers,
scoundrels, and liars. When cut loose from its anchor in
Christ, biblical texts have been used to justify polygamy, child
sacrifice, owning and beating slaves, subjugation of women,
burning of heretics, and the genocidal slaughter of enemies.
As Paul knew from his own violent, pre-Christian past, "the
letter [of the law] kills" (2 Corinthians 3:6). It is only as we
read the Scriptures in the light of the One who said, "I am
the way and the truth and the life" (John 14:6), that "the
Spirit gives life" (2 Corinthians 3:6), and accomplish their
holy purpose of "inerrantly revealing the will of God concerning us in all things necessary to our salvation."[5]

Third, *Wesleyans are "spiritual abolitionists":* that is, they
believe that holiness is not only an ideal for which to strive,
but *a present freedom from the tyranny of sin* to be experienced
and enjoyed through the indwelling presence of the Holy
Spirit. While most evangelicals, again reflecting Calvin's
theology, steadfastly maintain that there is no escape from
sinning in thought, word, and deed daily so long as we shall
live, Wesleyans rejoice in the "evangel"—the Good News—
that we can, by grace through faith, be "set free from sin" and
"become slaves to God." The purifying, renewing, and exhil-

arating "benefit" we reap "leads to holiness, and the result is eternal life" (Romans 6:22). We are not delivered from the *possibility* of sin or *temptations* to sin, but liberated from the *compulsion* to sin.

It is ironic that the very ones who so dogmatically defend the inerrancy of the Bible resist so passionately the overwhelming testimony of the Scriptures that believers can not only experience the forgiveness of sins, but *deliverance from the sin nature*. Jesus, who warned that "everyone who sins is a slave to sin," also promised that "if the Son sets you free, *you will be free indeed*" (John 8:34, 36, emphasis added). And what a marvelous freedom it is! John, the beloved apostle, affirms, "If we walk in the light, as he is in the light, we have fellowship with one another, and the blood of Jesus, his Son, purifies us from *all* sin" (1 John 1:7, emphasis added).[6] It is the propagation of this blessed liberating experience— "the doctrine and experience of entire sanctification"—that is the "special calling" of churches within the Wesleyan theological tradition.[7]

Notes:

1. *Manual,* Church of the Nazarene (Kansas City: Nazarene Publishing House, 2001), 14.

2. John Calvin, *Institutes of the Christian Religion,* John T. McNeill, ed., Ford Lewis Battles, trans. (Philadelphia: Westminster, 1960), 1, xvi, 3.

3. John Wesley, "Free Grace," *The Works of John Wesley* (London: Wesleyan Conference Office, 1872, reproduced by photo offset by the Nazarene Publishing House, Kansas City, Mo., n.d.), VII, 373-86.

4. Walter Wink, *Engaging the Powers* (Minneapolis: Fortress Press, 1992), 149.

5. *Manual,* Article IV, "The Holy Scriptures," 27.

6. See also Psalm 51; Matthew 5:43-48; Luke 6:31-38; John 14:26; 15:26; 16:7-14; 17; Acts 2; 15:8-9; Romans 6; 8; 12—13; Ephesians 1:3-5; 4—6; Colossians 3:1ff.; 1 Thessalonians 4:3-8; 5:22-23; 1 Peter 1:15-16; 1 John 3:1-10; 4:7-21; Revelation 21:27.

7. *Manual,* 14.

Scripture Cited: John 3:16-17; 5:39; 8:34, 36; 14:6; Romans 6:22; 2 Corinthians 3:6; 5:19; 1 John 1:7

13

THE PRESENT RELIGIOUS LANDSCAPE

BY STAN INGERSOL

One in three persons in the world were self-identified with the Christian faith in 1900. In the year 2000, the ratio remained one in three. The 60 million Christians living in North America in 1900 composed just under 11 percent of the world's Christian family in 1900. In 2000, about 216 million North Americans identified themselves with the Christian faith, representing . . . just under 11 percent of the world's total. In other words, the place of North American Christianity within the wider community of world Christians was roughly the same at both ends of the 20th century.[1]

On the surface, these statistics suggest that global Christianity's place in the world changed very little over the 20th century. But that conclusion would be wrong. In fact, dramatic changes occurred.

In 1900, only 1.6 percent of the world's Christians lived in Africa; but by 2000, the number of African Christians had soared from 8.8 million to over 346 million. At the dawn of the 21st century, Africa was the home of over 17.3 percent of the world's Christians.

In Asia, the number of Christians soared from under 21 million in 1900 to 303 million by 2001, or from 3.8 percent to 15 percent of the world Christian population.

Thus, Africa and Asia—the home of less than 6 percent of the Christian population in 1900—is now home to over 35 percent of Christians today. And their share is rising.

In 1900, Latin America claimed just under 11 percent of the world's Christians, but by 2000 it claimed nearly 24 percent, pushed by tremendous population growth in nations where some of the planet's most loyal Roman Catholics live.

These changes in Africa and Latin America bear witness to a clear trend that is reshaping the Christian world. In 1900, Africa and Latin America accounted for about 12.5 percent of all Christians. By 2005, these continents were the homes of 40 percent of all Christians. One of the most fundamental shifts in global Christianity over the last century was a shift in influence from the northern hemisphere to the southern hemisphere—a trend that continues even now.

For centuries, Christianity has been identified with Europe and North America, but the plane of Christian development today lies on an axis that runs from South America through Africa to Asia. Well over half of today's Christians are found along that axis. As Phillip Jenkins makes so clear in his book, *The Next Christendom,* we have long thought of the centers of Christian influence being Rome, Moscow, Canterbury, and New York City; but the emerging centers of world Christianity today are Seoul, Nairobi, Lagos, Rio de Janeiro, and Quito.

We will look at some people whose ministries in the late 20th century illustrate some of the overarching themes of the past century.

AN AGENT OF GLOBAL CHANGE

Over 66 percent of the world's Christians lived in Europe (including Russia) in 1900. By 2000, only 27 percent lived there. Christianity in Europe declined in the 20th century for several reasons. Two world wars and the rise and establishment of totalitarian regimes were part of the story.

Christianity was also eroded by Soviet communism's 70-year program of state-sponsored atheism designed to eradicate religious influence in Russian state and cultural affairs. This campaign, carried out at first in Russian schools, was extended into Soviet-occupied Eastern Europe after World War II.

In Western Europe, meanwhile, the centuries-old system of state-supported churches was challenged by a strong secular trend that eroded loyalty to the churches and to the Christian faith.

These larger realities shaped the life and ministry of the man who became known to the world as Pope John Paul II. He was born Karol Wojtyla in Wadowice, Poland, some 30 miles from Krakow. His ministry spanned over a half-century and was intertwined with the titanic struggle between the Christian churches in Eastern Europe and the communist campaign against them.

Karol Wojtlya was born in 1920. His mother died when he was nine. His father encouraged his studies, but died while Wojtlya was in college. A good student, he was also an athlete and enjoyed acting. He had a charisma that endeared him to other people. These traits all prepared him for the priesthood.

Germany invaded Poland in 1939, bringing war and foreign domination to his nation. Wojtyla was forced to work in a quarry. He entered an underground seminary in 1942 and was ordained to the ministry four years later. By that time, World War II had ended. Soviet troops occupied Poland and a communist regime was imposed on the Polish people.

The government was unable to suppress the church, although it actively discriminated against it. Wojtyla succeeded in earning two doctoral degrees in the 1950s—one in theology, the other in philosophy. He became a professor of ethics at a Catholic university in Lublin. In the face of communism's insistence that rational people had no use for God, Wojtyla used philosophy to argue the case for the truth of

Christian doctrine and to witness to the continuing relevance of the divine mystery of God in the modern world. His charisma and intellect won him a following.

In 1958, he was appointed auxiliary (or assistant) bishop to help the archbishop of Krakow. He was only 38. Five years later, he was elevated to archbishop. Throughout Wojtyla's years as bishop and archbishop, the Catholic Church became increasingly important in Polish resistance against the Communist Party. Though Poles were denied freedom of expression and assembly for any purposes that were clearly at odds with the Communist Party, the Church became a place where people could express themselves in ways that indicated their lack of sympathy with the Party and powers that governed them. At the Second Vatican Council in the early '60s, Wojtyla spoke out on behalf of freedom of religion—a conviction borne of the Polish church's situation under a Marxist regime. At Vatican II, Wojtyla wrote legislation that was approved by the Council and placed the Roman Catholic Church on the side of religious liberty for the first time.

In 1978, Wojtyla was elected to lead the Roman Catholic Church. The election came as a great surprise to him and to the world. He took the papal name of John Paul—the name of his immediate predecessor, who had served only a month—derived from the reforming popes John XXIII and Paul VI. John had convened the Second Vatican Council, which brought far-reaching changes to the Roman Catholic communion, while Paul had striven to implement the reforms. By taking the name John Paul II, Wojtyla underscored his intention to proceed in continuity with their work.

At 58, he was a young pope and energetic—still athletic and an avid skier. His election was a tremendous event in Poland, but it was meaningful also to other Slavic peoples behind the iron curtain. There was now a Slavic leader on the world stage, who championed democracy and religious freedom. Clearly, John Paul II's papacy would have consequences. The new pope visited Poland in 1979, speaking to large crowds—3.5 million on one occasion. The government did not welcome the visit, but felt compelled to accept it out of fear of the people; and the papal visit forged a link between the Polish church and a growing independent trade union known as Solidarity, which was challenging the Communist regime's exclusive rule.

The ministry of Jerzy Popieluszko, a priest in Warsaw, was a visible sign of this growing alliance between the church and the Solidarity trade unionists. Popieluszko preached to thousands, and from the pulpit, became an outspoken defender of Solidarity's rights. The police harassed him, and throughout 1984, he criticized the regime's oppression of the church and of the workers. Late that year, he was taken into police custody and never released. A few weeks later, his badly-beaten body was found. The martyrdom of Jerzy Popieluszko strengthened the resolve of Polish reformers.

Newsweek's Andrew Nagorski later wrote: "Everything about this pope was intense and some of it was subversive. When I was reporting on the fate of religion in Eastern and Central Europe, I became aware of the scope of his encouragement for the faithful in places like Ukraine and Czechoslovakia, where persecution was the norm. I talked with one of the Polish priests, dressed in civilian clothes, who traveled to parts of the Soviet Union to hold secret masses."[2]

The unraveling of the Soviet empire began in Poland. And while the downfall of European communism had several causes, the election of a Slavic pope who was one with the oppressed was one of the leading factors.

John Paul's papacy lasted 26 years. In the face of the West's materialistic culture and its embrace of secularism, he emphasized evangelization, revival within the Catholic Church, and the importance of vital Christian faith in an age of reason and secular influence. He became an inveterate world-traveler, visiting the Catholic faithful across the world. He wanted, especially, to stimulate young people to take faith seriously. At the time of John Paul's death in 2005, there were over 1 billion Roman Catholics, or 1 in every 6 people, and the Catholic Church accounted for half of all the world's Christians.

A LIFE OF SERVICE

Mother Teresa represents a different aspect of late 20th-century Christianity: the life of service that came to distinguish a growing segment of Christian thought and action.

Born in Albania in 1910 and named Agnes, she was deeply religious and interested in missions from her youth. She felt especially called to India, and joined the Irish Province of the Sisters of Loretto because they had work in Calcutta. She arrived in India in early 1929. She served her years as a novice in Darjeeling, at the foot of the Himalayas, and took vows in 1931, taking the name Teresa. She was sent to Calcutta to live in an enclosed convent and teach at a school for the children of the poor.

Her vision for a new ministry took shape in the bloody aftermath of India and Pakistan's independence in 1946, as violence broke out between Hindus and Muslims. Her call, as she increasingly understood it, was to serve Jesus "in the poorest of the poor."

In 1950, she became founder of a new religious order known as the Missionaries of Charity. One of its first ministries was to the destitute dying, who often lay in the streets. Teresa and her sisters began taking the dying off the streets and cleaning and caring for them. Soon ambulances also brought people to them. The Sister's hope was in the recovery of their wards, but if not, then at least the dignity of a humane death. "To me, each one is Christ—Christ in a distressing disguise," Mother Teresa told writer Eileen Egan. Egan continues: "It was in this spirit that the Missionaries of Charity were trained. In their vision, they saw divinity in each human person."[3] Doctors and nurses began volunteering time with them. The Missionaries of Charity also opened ministries of food for the poor, especially refugees, and they took in orphaned and abandoned children.

In 1960, the work was spread from Calcutta into other cities of India, and in time the order spread into other countries. By 1985, the Missionaries of Charity had 4,000 sisters in over 100 nations.

PROTESTANTISM'S CHANGING FACE

The face of Protestantism has been predominantly European and North American since the Reformation in the 16th century. That changed in the 20th century.

A central theme of Africa's 20th-century story is the conversion of its peoples from traditional African religions to monotheistic faiths—Christianity and Islam, with each faith now embracing over 40 percent of Africans.

Festo Kivengere's life illustrates the changing face of global Protestantism and the spread of Christianity in Africa.

Kivengere was born in Uganda in 1919. He grew up herding cattle like many other boys in rural East Africa. He attended a mission school, advanced to higher education, and became a schoolteacher. He was converted to Christ in high school and traveled with student evangelism teams, but backslid later. He was reclaimed as an adult, and in 1946, became a lay evangelist with the Church Missionary Society, the Church of England's mission arm. He played an important role in the East African revival. He served as an interpreter for Billy Graham, with whom he developed a lifelong friendship. Indeed, Kivengere was dubbed "the Billy Graham of Africa." This writer's mother traveled to Addis Ababa, Ethiopia, in 1964 to witness and participate in one of Kivengere's evangelistic crusades.

Kivengere was ordained in 1967. The Anglican Church was growing rapidly in Uganda through revival, and in 1972, Kivengere was elected as the first bishop for the newly-creat-

ed diocese of Kigezi. He was part of the new generation of
Christian leaders who were replacing the missionaries.

The murderous dictator, Idi Amin, then ruled Uganda
and initiated a concerted oppression of the churches, including the assassination of Kivengere's colleague, Bishop Luwum,
in 1977. Upon advice, Kivengere left Uganda until Amin was
deposed in 1979. Kivengere spent his months in exile traveling the globe, with an active speaking schedule. He returned
to Uganda as a staunch advocate on behalf of human rights.

Uganda remained in turmoil after Amin's reign. Kivengere sought reconciliation at all levels—between humans and
God, and between the divided members of the human family. He spoke out against the efforts of Amin's successor to
divide Ugandan Christians by turning Catholics and Protestants against each other. And in 1980, he was a cofounder of
African Evangelistic Enterprise, an organization dedicated
to evangelizing the whole continent. Through all, he earned
his other nickname, "Africa's Apostle of Love."

Kivengere died of leukemia in 1988. His spirit is nowhere
more evident than in his address, "The Cross and World
Evangelization," delivered to the International Congress on
World Evangelization at Lausanne, Switzerland, in 1974.

Kivengere preached: "It is in the Cross that the truth
becomes incarnate and reaches us where we are. It is the
Cross which encourages us to cross over the barriers of our
particular camps to meet God's world. The Cross of Christ
is the panacea for the deep troubles of the human race. It is
the hope of my beloved country [in] Africa, with all its con-
flicting problems. It is the panacea for the so-called richer
nations of the West, with their disturbing disintegrations of
lives in the midst of material plenty."[4]

THERE IS MORE TO THE STORY

The lives of these 20th-century Christians are a small
part of a tapestry that is now 2,000 years in the making.

That tapestry now includes pieces from all the inhabited continents. Since the time of the apostles, the church of Jesus Christ has lived to bear witness to God's love in this world. We have seen in this book how persons of faith have been faithful witnesses down through the generations. Now, the important question becomes for us: Where do you and I fit into this story?

The apostle Paul, in his theology of the Christian ecclesia as "the body of Christ" (1 Corinthians 12:27), makes clear that since Jesus' ascension, it is now the hands and feet of His followers that are God's hands and feet in the world. There are consequences to what we do, how we do it, and whether or not the Christian witness will be credible.

The story of the Christian church is our story. And what we add to it will become the story of our children and their children.

Notes:

1. These statistics are developed by statistician David Barrett and his associates, and they are updated and published annually. See "Status of Global Mission, 2005, in the Context of the 20th and 21st Centuries," *International Bulletin of Missionary Research,* vol. 29, No. 1 (January 2005): 29.

2. Andrew Nagorski, "Freedom Matters," *Newsweek* (April 11, 2005): 47.

3. Eileen Egan, "Mother Teresa, 87, Friend to Destitute, Dies in Calcutta," *National Catholic Reporter* (Sept. 19, 1997): insert, 3.

4. Festo Kivengere, "The Cross and World Evangelization," in J. D. Douglas, ed., *Let the Earth Hear His Voice* (Minneapolis: World Wide Publications, 1975), 404.

Scripture Cited: 1 Corinthians 12:27

ABOUT THE AUTHORS

Chapters 1, 4, 13

Dr. Stan Ingersol is a church historian and archivist for the Church of the Nazarene at its International Center in Kansas City, Missouri.

Chapters 2, 10

Dr. Diane Leclerc is professor of historical theology at Northwest Nazarene University, Nampa, Idaho.

Chapters 3, 5, 8, 12

Dr. C. S. Cowles is professor emeritus of Northwest Nazarene University, Boise, Idaho. He is currently an adjunct professor at Point Loma Nazarene University and Azusa Pacific University, both in southern California.

Chapters 6, 7

Dr. Carl M. Leth is chair of the religion department at Olivet Nazarene University, Bourbonnais, Illinois.

Chapters 9, 11

Dr. Floyd Cunningham is academic dean and professor of church history at Asia-Pacific Nazarene Theological Seminary in Kaytikling, Taytay, Philippines.